THE ART OF
PANTRY COOKING

RIZZOLI
NEW YORK

New York · Paris · London · Milan

THE ART OF
PANTRY COOKING
MEALS FOR FAMILY AND FRIENDS

RONDA CARMAN

PHOTOGRAPHY BY MATTHEW MEAD

Nothing brings people together like good food.
And a friend who offers you a meal also offers you their heart.
–*Ronda Carman*

To the Cooking Club:
Your recipes and generosity of spirit have inspired this book.

CONTENTS

INTRODUCTION

I have long had a love affair with cooking. From planning a feast for my family to reading cookbooks in bed to anticipating the next meal, each offers me endless joy. And yet, with all my enthusiasm, I began to find myself in the kitchen a little less often due to extensive travel. Then 2020 came along.

Out of a need for comfort and culinary creativity, I turned to the cherished cookbooks that I have collected over the years for inspiration. Like old friends, Sarah Leah Chase, Jacques Pépin, Patricia Wells, Betty Rosbottom, Julee Rosso, Sheila Lukins, Ina Garten, and others were waiting for me. I started by making a list of the recipes I had always wanted to attempt, challenging myself to make good use of my pantry staples. My first choice was a dinner of lasagna Bolognese with rich a béchamel sauce. The flavorful dish filled the entire house with aromatic warmth. As our family gathered around the table, I felt a huge sense of appreciation that we were all together.

During a time of not wanting to make too many trips to the supermarket, I was reminded that essential supplies are a must. Without key staples, cooking can be challenging. Having a well-stocked pantry allows you to easily create delicious and beautifully seasoned dishes. After many months of cooking, experimenting, and creating recipes, *The Art of Pantry Cooking* was born. Organized alphabetically, the pantry staples featured here are my foundations for preparing meals that reflect the way we cook and eat today. Each staple in this book is the basis for all of recipes that follow.

I have always felt that mealtimes are so much more than simply the act of eating— they offer us a way to connect with others. It was that very belief that inspired me to start The Cooking Club with Ronda Carman on Facebook. Within a few weeks there were over two thousand members. Strangers from around the world came together to share stories and recipes based on their own pantry items, and they continue to do so today. But more than simply posting pictures of what each member is cooking, baking, and eating, we are connecting.

As with the cooking group, it is my hope that this cookbook provides you with inspiration and simple pantry-based recipes to share with your family and friends. Whether you are experimenting in the kitchen, perfecting the classics, cooking for loved ones, or looking for a quick and satisfying weeknight dinner, this collection offers something for everyone.

PANTRY BASICS

When setting up a pantry, organize items in a way that allows for easy accessibility. Place like goods together so that you can find what you need or easily check an expiration date. Pantry basics will vary from person to person, and these are just a few of my personal favorite items.

BAKING: all-purpose flour, baking powder, baking soda, bittersweet baking chocolate, cocoa powder, cornmeal, cornstarch, espresso powder, nut butters, pure vanilla extract, semisweet chocolate, whole wheat flour

CANS AND JARS: anchovies, artichoke hearts, black beans, caperberries, capers, chickpeas, coconut milk, olives, pepperoncini peppers, San Marzano tomatoes, tomato paste, tomato sauce, tuna, white beans

CONDIMENTS AND SAUCES: Bragg liquid aminos, fish sauce, harissa paste, kecap manis, ketchup, mayonnaise, mustard, pesto, soy sauce, sriracha, Tabasco, Worcestershire sauce, XO sauce, yuzu juice

DRIED FRUITS: apricots, black raisins, cranberries, figs, golden raisins, medjool dates, prunes, sundried tomatoes

FREEZE-DRIED HERBS: Litehouse basil, chives, cilantro, oregano, parsley, thyme

GRAINS, STARCHES, AND DRIED LEGUMES: Arborio rice, basmati rice, bucatini, bulgur, cornmeal, couscous, farro, lasagna noodles, lentils, quinoa, oats, orzo, panko breadcrumbs, pappardelle, split peas, udon noodles

HERBS AND SPICES: Aleppo pepper, basil, bay leaves, black peppercorns, cayenne, cinnamon, cloves, curry powder, garlic powder, isot pepper, nutmeg, oregano, paprika, red pepper flakes, sumac, thyme, za'atar

NUTS: almonds, cashews, Marcona almonds, pecans, pine nuts, pistachios, roasted peanuts, sesame seeds, sunflower seeds, walnuts

OILS AND VINEGARS: apple cider vinegar, balsamic vinegar, canola oil, coconut oil, extra-virgin olive oil, ghee, grapeseed oil, red wine vinegar, rice vinegar, toasted sesame oil, white wine vinegar

SALT: fine sea salt, fleur de sel, kosher salt, sea salt flakes

STOCKS AND BROTHS: Better than Bouillon base, Kettle & Fire bone broth, Kitchen Basics broth and stock, Swanson bone broth

SWEETENERS: agave, dark brown sugar, granulated sugar, powdered sugar, honey, jam, light brown sugar, molasses

While the recipes in *The Art of Pantry Cooking* focus primarily on pantry goods, it is also important to have refrigerator staples on hand. My basics include cured meats, eggs, feta, fresh herbs, lemons, limes, milk, nut milk, Parmigiano Reggiano, plain Greek yogurt, ricotta, salted and unsalted butter, and sour cream.

ALMONDS

FROM SPICED MOROCCAN ALMOND SOUP TO VEGAN HOT CHOCOLATE, almonds are truly a workhorse in the kitchen. Often referred to as a nut, the almond is actually the edible seed of the almond tree. Naturally sweet, almonds are perfect for baking and add a unique flavor and aroma to a wide range of desserts. However, their culinary prowess should not be limited to baked goods. Both raw and roasted almonds are delicious in pesto, soups, salads, and meatloaf.

Versatility aside, almonds are renowned for their health benefits. Packed with plant-based protein, almonds contain high levels of antioxidants. Roasted almonds will last for up to one year in an airtight container in the refrigerator or freezer.

BUYING AND STORING ALMONDS

During the holidays I love to keep unshelled almonds in cut-glass bowls along with brass nutcrackers for my guests. However, for cooking I use shelled almonds.

Due to their high fat content, almonds can turn rancid, especially at warm temperatures, if they are not stored correctly. Once packaged almonds are opened, place them in an airtight container or resealable bag. Store them in a cool, dry, dark place and use within three months. If storing in the freezer, make certain that the container is tightly sealed to prevent odor absorption, as almonds do tend to take on the odors of other foods.

Both raw and blanched almonds are sold whole, sliced, slivered, halved, diced, and chopped. For the freshest flavor, purchase almonds whole and chop or slice them as needed before each use.

TOASTING ALMONDS

Toasting almonds deepens their flavor and adds an extra crunch to recipes.

Toasting almonds on the stove: Place the almonds in a dry skillet over medium-low heat. Toast, stirring occasionally, until light brown and fragrant, 3 to 5 minutes.

Toasting almonds in the oven: Preheat the oven to 350°F. Spread the almonds on a baking sheet and toast until golden and fragrant, 7 to 8 minutes. This method is preferred for quantities over 1 cup.

ROMESCO

Makes 1½ cups

Similar to a pesto, romesco is a rich Spanish sauce of roasted red peppers that is thickened with toasted almonds and bread. Traditionally it is served with grilled fish, chicken, or steak. I love it just as much with raw vegetables and flatbread.

INGREDIENTS

¼ cup extra-virgin olive oil

½ cup torn small pieces crusty bread

½ cup blanched whole unsalted almonds

One 12-ounce jar roasted
  red bell peppers, drained

1 tablespoon red wine or sherry vinegar

1 tablespoon smoked paprika

½ teaspoon hot paprika

1 teaspoon ground cumin

½ teaspoon red pepper flakes

6 cloves garlic

¼ cup loosely packed flat-leaf parsley leaves

Kosher salt and freshly ground
  black pepper to taste

Fresh thyme sprig for garnish

In a medium skillet, heat the oil over medium-high heat. Add the pieces of bread and almonds. Toss frequently to coat the bread. Toast the bread until it starts to turn a golden brown and the almonds become fragrant, about 3 minutes. Remove the skillet from the heat and allow the mixture to cool.

Transfer the bread and almonds to a food processor or blender. Add the red peppers, vinegar, paprikas, cumin, pepper flakes, garlic, and parsley. Pulse until smooth, 1 to 2 minutes. Taste and season with salt and pepper as needed. Pulse to combine. Garnish with fresh thyme, and serve immediately, or cover and refrigerate for up to 3 days.

HARISSA-SPICED MOROCCAN CAULIFLOWER AND ALMOND SOUP

Serves 2 as a main course or 4 as a starter

In this warm soup, the North African flavors combine with the pureed cauliflower and toasted almonds to create a rich, satisfying meal. Pair with a buttery Chardonnay and a loaf of crusty bread or garlic naan. Sriracha hot sauce can be substituted for harissa paste.

INGREDIENTS

2 tablespoons extra-virgin olive oil

1 small yellow onion, finely diced

½ teaspoon ground cinnamon

½ teaspoon ground cumin

½ teaspoon ground coriander

1 tablespoon harissa paste

1 large head cauliflower, cut into small florets

1½ cups vegetable or chicken stock

1¼ cups almond flakes, toasted

¼ cup half-and-half

1 small baguette, cut into ¾-inch cubes and toasted

Freshly ground black pepper to taste

Heat the oil in a large stockpot over medium heat. Add the onion and sauté until very soft, 5 to 7 minutes. Add the cinnamon, cumin, coriander, and harissa paste and cook, stirring constantly, for 2 minutes. Add the cauliflower florets, stock, and 1 cup of the toasted almond flakes. Cover and cook until the cauliflower is tender, about 20 minutes.

Puree the soup with an immersion blender until smooth. (If you don't have an immersion blender, you can let the soup cool, then puree the solids in a food processor fitted with the metal blade and return them to the pot) Reheat the soup in the stockpot. Add the half-and-half and mix thoroughly.

To serve, ladle the warm soup into bowls and top with the remaining toasted almonds and the toasted bread cubes. Season with pepper as needed.

SUMMER SQUASH AND CARROT SALAD WITH SHAVED RICOTTA SALATA AND ALMONDS

Serves 4 to 6

This salad, adapted from the recipe of *New York Times* food editor Alexa Weibel, is my go-to in the summer. Raw squash and carrots pair perfectly with crunchy almonds. Punctuated with caper brine and lemon juice, it is bright, salty, and flavorful. Pick up a rotisserie chicken and serve this salad as a side for a quick dinner, or on its own as a light lunch.

INGREDIENTS

2 tablespoons capers in brine

3 tablespoons extra-virgin olive oil

1 shallot, minced

2 tablespoons freshly squeezed lemon juice

3 cloves garlic, minced

¼ teaspoon red pepper flakes

Kosher salt and freshly ground black pepper to taste

2 medium yellow squash

2 medium zucchini

2 large carrots

¼ cup fresh basil leaves

½ cup roasted salted almonds, roughly chopped

½ cup shaved strips of ricotta salata

2 lemon wedges, optional

Drain the capers over a bowl, reserving 2 teaspoons of the brine. Roughly chop the drained capers. In a small bowl, whisk together the oil, shallot, capers and reserved brine, lemon juice, garlic, and red pepper flakes. Season with salt and pepper to taste. Set the dressing aside.

Slice the yellow squash, zucchini, and carrots lengthwise into ¼-inch-thick batons. Toss the vegetables with the dressing. Arrange the dressed vegetables in a serving bowl or on a platter. Scatter the basil leaves, almonds, and ricotta salata on top. Garnish with lemon wedges, if desired, and serve immediately.

ANCHOVIES

ANCHOVIES ARE MAGICAL. Though small in size, this versatile little fish is big in flavor and deserves a spot in your pantry. However, mention the word anchovy and most people fain disdain. Perhaps a bad pizza or a subpar Caesar salad comes to mind. Such a shame, because the anchovy is an awesome oily fish.

Anchovies fresh out of the sea are quite mild in flavor. Once they are salt-cured and packed in good olive oil, they become intensely rich. When they are stirred into a pasta sauce or stew, their pungent flavor adds a savory note that amplifies the other ingredients.

As a general rule, I favor anchovies that have been cured for three to six months. When the filets age, their flavor becomes more complex, but aging is not necessarily better since the flesh breaks down and becomes less tender.

JARS OR TINS

Anchovy filets come packed in both tins and jars. Which is best is a personal preference. Some anchovy enthusiasts believe that the tins protect the integrity of the filets because they store them flat. Others swear by jars. I personally love both Merro and Ortiz anchovies, which both come in jars.

STORING

Anchovies are extremely sensitive to heat. Once a jar or tin of anchovies is opened, the filets must be properly stored. If using tinned anchovies, transfer the leftovers to a glass container or jar, cover the filets with olive oil, firmly seal the lid, and store in the refrigerator. The filets need to be completely submerged in the oil so that they do not spoil. If the oil is low in a jar of anchovies, fill the container with more oil.

ANCHOVY PAIRINGS

Food pairings: For me, anchovies with a slice of Manchego cheese and a glass of fino sherry is a perfect pairing. Toasted bread rubbed with a slice of garlic and topped with a tomato slice and a single anchovy filet is equally sublime.

Wine pairings: A remarkable thing happens when you flavor dishes with anchovies—their intensity grows. One might normally pair fish with a white wine but consider giving red a try.

WINES TO CONSIDER

Cinsault: Typically paired with escargot, this punchy, fruit-forward wine stands up well to anchovies.

Gamay: Treasured for its delicate aromas and subtle earthy notes, this grape pairs well with many types of food, including fish.

Pinot noir: Commonly referred to as the "noble grape," this wine is loved for its red fruit, spice aroma, and smooth finish.

ANCHOVY–CARAMELIZED ONION BUTTER

Makes ½ cup

If you consider anchovies to be too salty, try mixing them with caramelized onions and whipped butter. This compound butter has a wonderful sweetness interspersed with a slight saltiness, and the anchovies melt pleasantly into the background. This butter is great atop a steak or spread it on a slice of bread hot from the oven.

INGREDIENTS

5 anchovy filets in oil
I tablespoon sugar
I large yellow onion, diced
I stick (8 tablespoons) unsalted butter, at room temperature

Reserve 1 tablespoon of the oil from the filets. Drain the filets, dice them, and set aside. Heat the reserved anchovy oil and the sugar in a large skillet over medium-high for 1 minute, stirring. Make sure the sugar does not caramelize. Add the onions and reduce the heat to medium-low. Cook, stirring often, until the onions are caramelized and soft, about 45 minutes.

Add the diced anchovy filets to the onion mixture. Remove from the heat and allow the onion mixture to cool completely.

Whip the butter with a hand mixer until light and fluffy. When the onion mixture is completely cool (you do not want to melt the butter), add it to the butter and fold until well combined. Using parchment paper or plastic wrap, roll the butter into a 2-inch-diameter cylinder and wrap tightly. The butter will keep in the refrigerator for up to 5 days.

ANCHOVY TOAST WITH BUTTER AND TOMATOES

Serves 4 as a light main course

This toast is easy to assemble and loaded with simple yet explosive flavors. Serve it on a large platter as an appetizer or with a green salad for a light dinner.

INGREDIENTS

12 ¼- to ½-inch baguette slices

1 large clove garlic, halved

6 tablespoons unsalted butter, at room temperature

3 small Roma tomatoes, thinly sliced

12 anchovy filets, drained and rinsed

2 tablespoons minced fresh thyme leaves

Red pepper flakes to taste

Fleur de sel to taste, optional

Adjust an oven rack 6 inches away from the broiler. Turn the broiler to high. Arrange the baguette slices in a single layer on a rimmed baking sheet. Broil until the bread is browned, 1 to 2 minutes. Flip the slices to broil the other side for 1 additional minute. Remove from the oven.

While the bread slices are still hot, carefully rub both sides with garlic. Allow the bread to cool for 1 minute. Spread about ½ tablespoon of butter on each slice. Top each buttered slice with a tomato slice and an anchovy filet. Sprinkle each with ½ teaspoon thyme, red pepper flakes, and fleur de sel, if using. Serve immediately.

PASTA PUTTANESCA

Serves 4 to 6

Let's get this out of the way. The translation of puttanesca is "of, relating to, or characteristic of a prostitute" (from the *Oxford English Dictionary*). The name is often said to have originated because the dish was quick enough to make in between appointments. Others say this Neapolitan dish smelled so good while cooking, it would lure clients in from the street. Either way pasta puttanesca, which typically includes tomatoes, olive oil, olives, capers, garlic, oregano, red pepper flakes, and, of course, anchovies, is one of my favorite dishes and can be prepared in minutes.

INGREDIENTS

¼ cup extra-virgin olive oil

6 large cloves garlic, finely chopped

One 28-ounce can crushed tomatoes (preferably Mutti brand)

½ cup Kalamata olives, pitted and halved

6 anchovy filets, drained, rinsed, and roughly chopped

3 tablespoons capers, drained

1 tablespoon finely chopped fresh or freeze-dried oregano

1 teaspoon red pepper flakes

Kosher salt and freshly ground black pepper to taste

1 pound bucatini or other long pasta

2 tablespoons roughly chopped flat-leaf parsley leaves

1 cup freshly grated Parmigiano Reggiano

Heat the oil in a large saucepan over medium-low heat. Add the garlic and sauté until fragrant, about 1 minute, taking care not to burn the garlic. Add the tomatoes, olives, anchovies, capers, oregano, and red pepper flakes. Raise the heat to medium-high and simmer until the sauce thickens and the tomatoes easily break with a wooden spoon, 8 to 10 minutes. Season to taste with salt and pepper.

While the sauce is simmering, bring a large pot of water to a boil, salt it to taste, and cook the pasta until tender but still firm to the bite in the center. Drain the pasta and return it to the same pot in which it cooked. Add the sauce and parsley. Toss over very low heat until the pasta is completely coated, about 2 minutes. Serve in individual bowls and top each serving with Parmigiano Reggiano.

ARTICHOKE
HEARTS

TRADER JOE'S®

Marinated

GRILLED
ARTICHOKE
HALVES

NET. WT. 12 OZ (340g)   DR. WT. 7.5 OZ (215g)

AS FAR AS VEGETABLES GO, THE ARTICHOKE IS AMONG THE MOST visually fascinating. I often wonder who the first daring soul was to tackle eating this species of thistle. Not knowing that a creamy, fleshly bottom existed, or that a succulent meaty heart awaited, it was certainly an act of bravery in my book.

There is no question that fresh artichokes can be intimidating to process and prepare. And while I am not one to shy away from the task, I do keep a stockpile of both canned and jarred artichoke hearts. They are perfect for cooking and offer a year-round easy alternative.

The mild flavor and buttery texture of artichoke hearts make them a great addition to salads, pastas, and dips. Additionally, they are wonderful roasted with a little olive oil or tossed with hearts of palm and a vinaigrette for a mixed heart salad.

CANS OR JARS

Canned artichoke hearts are usually packed in water, salt, and citric acid to preserve their color. To reduce the amount of sodium in canned artichoke hearts, rinse them in cold water prior to use. Refrigerate the unused portion in a covered glass or plastic container for up to four days.

Jarred artichoke hearts are most often marinated in oil and herbs. Their bold flavor adds an instant boost to salads and grain bowls. They are the perfect complement to an antipasto platter. You can also eat them straight from the jar as a snack.

EASY MENUS

Antipasto platter: Pile artichoke hearts, salami, prosciutto, capocollo, peppadew peppers, cheeses, mixed olives, grilled vegetables, Marcona almonds, and flatbread on a platter for an im-promptu gathering.

Roasted artichoke hearts: Roasting vegetables brings out their natural sweetness and adds a touch of crispness. Toss canned artichoke hearts with a little extra-virgin olive oil and roast them in a 375°F oven for 30 minutes. Serve with a garlicky aioli for a delicious and simple side dish.

Quick weeknight pasta: Sauté crushed garlic in extra-virgin olive oil. Toss in diced tomatoes, a few fresh herbs, and a splash of red wine. Bring to a simmer, then toss with hot pasta, marinated artichokes, and grated Parmigiano Reggiano.

ARTICHOKES AND WINE ARE NOT FOES

Artichokes are notoriously difficult to pair with wine due to a naturally occurring chemical in them called cynarin, an element that makes everything you eat taste sweet. When wine encounters cynarin on one's palate it enhances any natural sweetness in the wine. To properly pair wine with an artichoke, select a wine that is bone dry, light, crisp, acidic, and without oak.

WINES TO CONSIDER

Fino: The driest, most saline style of sherry, this pale white sherry wine pairs perfectly with a raw artichoke salad.

Grüner Veltliner: Produced primarily in Austria, Hungary, Slovakia, and the Czech Republic, this dry white wine's primary flavors are lime, lemon, and grapefruit, with an herbaceous white pepper note.

Sauvignon blanc: The minerality and salinity of this wine pairs well with the earthiness of artichokes.

SHERRY-BRAISED CHICKEN WITH ARTICHOKE HEARTS

Serves 4 to 6

I updated this super easy recipe from a 1960s newspaper clipping that my mother had saved. I changed it by substituting a douse of good sherry and dry vermouth for red wine or cooking wine. The chicken, mushrooms, and paprika combination harkens back to the comfort foods of my childhood—albeit in a more sophisticated version.

INGREDIENTS

1½ teaspoons sea salt

1 teaspoon freshly ground black pepper, plus more to taste

1 teaspoon smoked paprika

One 3-pound whole chicken, cut into pieces

6 tablespoons unsalted butter

2 tablespoons dry vermouth

2 cups quartered cremini mushrooms

2 tablespoons unbleached all-purpose flour

⅔ cup chicken stock

2 tablespoons Manzanilla sherry

Kosher salt to taste

2 cups canned artichoke hearts, rinsed, drained, and halved

Flat-leaf parsely for garnish

Preheat the oven to 375°F.

In a small bowl mix together the sea salt, 1 teaspoon pepper, and paprika. Sprinkle the mixture on all sides of the chicken and set aside.

Melt 4 tablespoons of the butter in a large skillet over medium-high heat. Brown the chicken on all sides, working in batches if needed. Transfer the chicken to a large Dutch oven and set aside.

Deglaze the skillet with the vermouth, scraping up any browned bits from the bottom of the pan. Lower the heat and add the remaining 2 tablespoons butter. When the butter starts to foam add the mushrooms and sauté until softened, 3 to 4 minutes. Sprinkle the mushrooms with flour and stir. Add the chicken broth and the sherry in a thin stream while stirring. Simmer and stir for an additional 2 minutes. Season to taste with kosher salt and pepper.

Pour the mushroom and sherry sauce over the chicken. Wedge the artichoke hearts between the chicken pieces. Cover and cook until the chicken reaches an internal temperature of 165°F, 50 to 55 minutes. To serve, place the chicken pieces on a large platter and top with the artichoke hearts, mushrooms, juices, and flat-leaf parsley.

ARTICHOKE HEARTS WITH LEMON ORZO AND TUNA

Serves 4

The unexpected balance of flavors in this dish provides an alternative to standard weeknight pasta. Sundried tomatoes marry magically with artichoke hearts and oil-packed jarred tuna.

INGREDIENTS

½ teaspoon kosher salt, plus more to taste

1½ cups orzo

1 tablespoon extra-virgin olive oil

1 red onion, finely diced

⅓ cup dry white wine

One 14-ounce can artichoke hearts, drained and quartered

½ cup oil-packed sundried tomatoes, drained and thinly sliced

One 7-ounce jar tuna in olive oil, drained

¼ cup sour cream

¼ cup freshly squeezed lemon juice

Freshly ground black pepper to taste

Basil leaves for garnish

Bring a large pot of water to a boil and salt it to taste. Add the orzo and cook at a high simmer, stirring occasionally, until al dente, 8 to 10 minutes. Drain well and set aside.

Heat the oil in a large skillet over medium-high heat. Add the onion and sauté until soft, 7 to 8 minutes. Season with ½ teaspoon salt. Add the wine and lower the heat. Allow the wine to reduce by half, about 5 minutes. Add the artichoke hearts and sundried tomatoes. Cook until tender and heated through, 2 to 3 minutes. Turn off the heat and gently stir in the tuna.

Transfer the orzo to a large bowl and toss with the sour cream and lemon juice. Add the artichoke and tuna mixture. Season with salt and pepper. Toss gently to combine. Adjust the salt and pepper, then garnish with basil leaves and serve.

BULGUR

BULGUR WHEAT, A STAPLE INGREDIENT in many Middle Eastern and Mediterranean cuisines, is best known for its leading role in the popular grain salad tabbouleh. Arab, Israeli, Egyptian, and Roman civilizations record eating bulgur as early as 1000 BCE.

And while many whole grains are notorious for their lengthy cooking times, bulgur is an exception. This nutty-tasting ancient food is easy to make and quick-cooking. It is perfect in salads, soups, and side dishes. Not only is bulgur delicious, but it can also easily be a substitute for rice, couscous, barley, or quinoa.

WHAT IS BULGUR WHEAT?

Bulgur is cracked whole-grain kernels of wheat that are parboiled and dried before packaging. As a result, it cooks much more quickly than whole wheatberries but offers a similarly chewy texture.

GRIND SIZE

Bulgur is numbered by the coarseness of the grind. A fine or medium bulgur is great for tabbouleh or breakfast porridge. The coarser varieties are perfect for adding a hearty texture to soups and pilafs.

Number 1

Fine: The smallest grind is similar in appearance to fine couscous.

Number 2

Medium: The most widely available, this type is similar in size to sesame seeds.

Number 3

Coarse: Slightly larger than medium grind, this works in most recipes.

Number 4

Extra coarse: With the largest pieces, this resembles steel-cut oats in size and is often used in pilafs.

STORAGE

Store bulgur wheat as you would any whole grain, in an airtight container protected from moisture, light, and heat. In the pantry, bulgur should stay fresh for up to two years. Freezer storage can double the shelf life. Cooked bulgur can be stored in an airtight container in the refrigerator for up to three days.

BULGUR IN FOODS AROUND THE WORLD

In India, bulgur is mixed with milk and sugar to create a soft porridge.

In the Lebanese Republic, bulgur soup infused with mint olive oil is a refreshing and filling dish.

Burghul bi dfeen is an old Middle Eastern dish loaded with beef cubes, bulgur, chickpeas, pearl onions, and seven spices (allspice, black pepper, cinnamon, cloves, coriander, ginger, and nutmeg). It is often served with plain yogurt.

Kibbeh, the national dish of Syria, are tasty bulgur croquettes filled with minced meat, nuts, and spices. Bulgur di Jaram, another popular Syrian dish, is a simple one-pot meal of bulgur and roast chicken.

Asure or ashura, also known as Noah's ark pudding, is a traditional Turkish sweet dish made with bulgur, fruit, honey, and nuts. Some claim that it is the world's oldest dessert.

LEMON-BULGUR RICOTTA PANCAKES

Serves 4

These lovely lemony pancakes were inspired by cookbook author Mark Bittman. Thanks to the ricotta, they are substantial yet remain light and fluffy. Bursting with blueberries, lemon zest, cloves, and cinnamon, they are delicious straight off the griddle.

INGREDIENTS

½ cup fine or medium (number 1 or number 2) bulgur

½ teaspoon plus 1 pinch kosher salt

1¼ cups boiling water

1 cup whole-milk ricotta

1 cup sour cream

3 large eggs

1 tablespoon finely grated lemon zest

½ teaspoon finely grated orange zest

1 cup whole wheat flour

3 tablespoons sugar

1 teaspoon ground cinnamon

¼ teaspoon baking soda

⅛ teaspoon ground cloves

½ cup fresh blueberries, plus more for serving

Vegetable oil or coconut oil for frying

Honey, maple syrup, or powdered sugar for serving

Combine the bulgur, pinch of salt, and boiling water in a medium bowl. Stir once and let sit until the bulgur is tender, 20 to 25 minutes. If any water remains, wrap the bulgur in cheesecloth or place it in a fine-mesh strainer and press down on the bulgur to release any residual water.

In a medium bowl, beat together the ricotta, sour cream, eggs, and lemon and orange zests. In another medium bowl, combine the flour, sugar, cinnamon, baking soda, cloves, and remaining ½ teaspoon salt. Fold the dry ingredients into the ricotta mixture using a siicone spatula, blending well but not beating. A few lumps are okay. Gently fold in the bulgur and ½ cup blueberries.

Place a large griddle or skillet over medium heat. When a few drops of water sizzle on the surface on contact, add a thin layer of oil. For each pancake, spoon ¼ cup batter onto the skillet.

Cook until bubbles form on top, 2 to 3 minutes. Carefully flip the pancakes and cook until golden brown, another 2 minutes. Transfer to a platter, cover loosely with aluminum foil, and keep warm in the oven. Continue with the remaining batter, oiling the skillet or griddle as needed between batches. Serve with extra blueberries and honey, maple syrup, or powdered sugar.

HEARTY TOMATO SOUP WITH BULGUR

Serves 4 to 6

I love soup and could eat it every day. I am always on the lookout for interesting varieties, and this recipe certainly fits the bill. A chilled version of this soup by Diane Kochilas, one of the world's foremost experts in Greek and Mediterranean cuisine, inspired food writer Martha Rose Shulman, who came up with a new twist. I have added a few touches of my own to create a simple, satisfying soup. For a variation, try it with spinach. Toss in a few handfuls and let it wilt before serving, or mix in thick cubes of white fish at the end and allow them to cook through.

INGREDIENTS

2 tablespoons extra-virgin olive oil,
   plus more for drizzling
2 medium yellow onions, finely chopped
1 teaspoon kosher salt, plus more to taste
¼ teaspoon red pepper flakes
4 cloves garlic, minced
One 28-ounce can chopped tomatoes
   and their juices

1 tablespoon tomato paste
1 teaspoon sugar
½ cup coarse (number 3) bulgur
1 cup dry white wine
4 cups vegetable or chicken stock
Freshly ground black pepper to taste
¼ cup chopped flat-leaf parsley leaves
½ cup crumbled feta

Heat the 2 tablespoons oil in a heavy stockpot over medium heat. Add the onions, 1 teaspoon salt, and red pepper flakes. Cook, stirring often, until the onion is very soft, 8 to 10 minutes. Stir in the garlic and cook until fragrant, 30 seconds. Stir in the tomatoes and their juices, tomato paste, and sugar. Bring to a simmer. Cook, stirring occasionally, until the tomatoes have reduced and broken down, about 10 minutes.

Transfer half of the tomato mixture to a bowl. Use an immersion blender to coarsely puree the tomato mixture in the pot, then return the tomato mixture that hasn't been pureed to the pot. Add the bulgur, wine, and stock. Season with salt and pepper to taste. Bring to a boil on high. Reduce the heat to medium-low, cover, and simmer until the bulgur is soft and the flavors meld, about 25 minutes. The soup will become thick and fragrant as it cooks. Adjust salt and pepper, if needed.

Ladle the soup into bowls. Sprinkle with parsley and feta, and drizzle with olive oil.

BULGUR WITH HALLOUMI AND ROASTED SWEET POTATOES

Serves 4

Roasted sweet potatoes and pomegranate molasses put an autumnal spin on tabbouleh. The mild, nutty flavor of bulgur pairs well with the roasted sweet potatoes, while the halloumi and dry-cured black olives offer a pleasant saltiness.

INGREDIENTS

2 medium sweet potatoes, peeled and diced

1 tablespoon grapeseed oil

1 tablespoon pomegranate molasses

1½ teaspoons kosher salt

1½ teaspoons freshly ground black pepper

1¾ cups coarse (number 2 or 3) bulgur

½ cup finely chopped flat-leaf parsley leaves

½ cup finely chopped fresh mint leaves

¼ cup finely chopped red onion

2 tablespoons finely grated orange zest

¼ cup plus 1 tablespoon extra-virgin olive oil, plus more for drizzling

¼ cup freshly squeezed orange juice

2 tablespoons freshly squeezed lemon juice

1 tablespoon red wine vinegar

1 clove garlic, minced

One 8.8-ounce package halloumi cheese, cut into 1-inch pieces

1 cup oil-cured black olives, pitted

1 teaspoon fresh thyme leaves

½ teaspoon red pepper flakes

Fresh sprigs of mint for garnish

Preheat the oven to 400°F.

In a large bowl, toss the sweet potatoes with the grapeseed oil, molasses, 1 teaspoon salt, and ½ teaspoon pepper.

Place the potatoes on a parchment-lined baking sheet and roast until very tender and gently caramelized, about 30 minutes. Stir the potatoes once halfway through roasting.

While the potatoes are roasting, place 3½ cups water in a medium saucepan and bring to a boil. Add the bulgur and lower the heat to a simmer. Simmer for 8 minutes, stirring occasionally. Remove the bulgur from the heat, cover, and let it sit for 10 minutes. Drain any excess water from the bulgur and fluff the grains with a fork. Set aside and allow to cool slightly.

When the potatoes are cooked, transfer them to a large mixing bowl. Add the cooked bulgur, parsley, mint, onion, and orange zest. In a small bowl whisk together the ¼ cup oil, orange

and lemon juices, vinegar, garlic, the remaining ½ teaspoon salt, and the remaining 1 teaspoon pepper. Add the dressing to the potatoes and bulgur. Toss well to combine and set aside.

In a cast-iron or nonstick skillet large enough to hold the cheese in a single layer, heat the remaining 1 tablespoon oil over medium heat. Once hot, add the halloumi. Cook the cheese undisturbed until it starts to develop a deep golden brown underneath, about 2 minutes. Using a thin flexible spatula, flip the cheese and cook until both sides are golden brown. Remove from the heat and add the olives, thyme, and red pepper flakes.

Arrange the dressed potato and bulgur mixture on a large platter. Top with the halloumi-olive mixture. Drizzle with oil, if desired, garnish with fresh mint, and serve.

OPEN-FACED BLACK BEAN BULGUR BURGERS WITH ZESTY LEMONGRASS MAYONNAISE

Serves 4

Adapted from a *Gourmet* recipe by Andrea Albin, these tasty burgers will satisfy vegetarians and meat-eaters alike. Made with beans, walnuts, warm spices, and bulgur, they are a welcome change from regular veggie options. A zesty lemongrass mayonnaise and toasted multigrain bread for serving as open-faced sandwiches elevate them further.

INGREDIENTS

2 tablespoons extra-virgin olive oil

¾ teaspoon kosher salt

½ cup chopped yellow onion

½ cup coarse (number 2 or 3) bulgur

1 cup canned black beans, rinsed and drained

1 tablespoon soy sauce

1 cup walnuts

3 cloves garlic, coarsely chopped

½ cup flat-leaf parsley leaves

1 teaspoon ground cumin

¼ teaspoon ground cayenne pepper

½ teaspoon freshly ground black pepper

½ cup mayonnaise

1 tablespoon chili sauce

½ tablespoon bruised and finely minced lemongrass

Zest and freshly squeezed juice of 1 lime

4 tablespoons soft goat cheese

4 slices multigrain bread, toasted

Sliced tomatoes and arugula for topping

In a heavy saucepan over medium heat, warm 1 tablespoon of the olive oil and ¼ teaspoon of the salt. Add the onion and cook, stirring occasionally, until golden, 5 to 7 minutes. Add the bulgur and 1 cup water and stir to combine. Lower the heat and cook, uncovered, until the water is completely absorbed, 15 to 20 minutes.

Once the bulgur is cooked, use a slotted spoon to transfer it to a food processor fitted with a metal blade. Add the black beans, soy sauce, walnuts, garlic, parsley, cumin, cayenne, the remaining ½ teaspoon salt, and the black pepper and pulse until the bulgur mixture is finely chopped and processed, about 1 minute. Scrape down the sides as needed.

Divide the mixture into four equal portions and form into rounded patties. Place the patties on a plate and chill for at least 10 minutes.

While the patties chill, stir together the mayonnaise, chili sauce, lemongrass, lime zest, and lime juice.

Heat the remaining 1 tablespoon oil in a 12-inch heavy skillet over medium heat. Add the patties and cook, carefully turning once, until golden brown on both sides, about 8 to 10 minutes total.

Spread 1 tablespoon of soft goat cheese on each slice of bread. Top each with a warm patty. Top each patty with a dollop of mayonnaise, a tomato slice or two, and arugula. Serve the burgers open-faced.

CAPERS

CAPERS SEEM TO FALL INTO the same love-it-or-hate-it category as anchovies. Yet when you use capers in the right dish, they elevate the flavor. A wonderful kitchen staple, these tiny buds add a salty, briny bite to most fish dishes, pastas, stews, sauces, and salads.

The immature, unripe, green flower buds of the caper bush are often associated with Mediterranean cuisines. Nevertheless, this plant is cultivated in Morocco, Spain, Asia, and Australia.

TYPES OF CAPERS

Capers are sold by size, with buds ranging from very tiny to the size of a small olive. Normally, the smaller the caper, the more delicate the texture and flavor. The smallest caper is labeled "nonpareil." Translated from French, it means no equal. Nonpareil capers have a delicate taste, whereas larger capers are more acidic and should be used sparingly. Because large capers are also very potent when eaten whole, they should be chopped before using.

STORING CAPERS

Capers are never used fresh. Instead, they are preserved in one of two ways: in brine or salt. How they are preserved determines the way they should be stored. Brine-packed capers should always be completely submerged in their brine. Open jars will keep for six months in the refrigerator. Unopened jars can be stored in a dark, dry pantry for up to three years, although it is always best to check the expiration date.

Salt-packed capers can be stored at room temperature for up to six months and must be rinsed several times in cold water prior to use. Both brine-packed and salt-packed capers should be stored in an airtight container. Any foul odor or discoloration are signs that the capers have gone bad and should be discarded immediately.

WAYS TO USE CAPERS

Salads: A few teaspoons of capers tossed into a bowl of leafy greens add texture and a pop of briny flavor. They are also great mixed in vinaigrettes. For a vegetarian Caesar salad dressing, substitute capers for the anchovies.

Eggs: Fold capers into omelets, scrambled eggs, and frittatas. For a different twist on deviled eggs, incorporate a few capers in place of paprika for the crowning touch.

Oysters: Capers are a wonderful topper for freshly opened oysters. They are also delicious mixed into a mignonette sauce.

PASTA WITH CAPERS, PANKO BREADCRUMBS, AND SARDINES

Serves 4 to 6

This classic Sicilian-style pasta dish varies a bit from kitchen to kitchen, but the basic ingredients remain the same—capers, sardines, parsley, lemon, and pasta. Even if you do not like sardines, I urge you to give this pasta a try; it just might change your mind. A fabulous combination of flavors, this dish is both hearty and easy to make.

INGREDIENTS

¼ teaspoon kosher salt, plus more for pasta cooking water and to taste

¼ cup extra-virgin olive oil

½ cup panko breadcrumbs

I medium yellow onion, finely diced

½ teaspoon freshly ground black pepper, plus more to taste

I teaspoon finely grated lemon zest

2 tablespoons drained capers

Two 4-ounce cans sardines in extra-virgin olive oil, drained, boned, and coarsely chopped

I pound bucatini, spaghetti, or other long pasta

½ cup chopped flat-leaf parsley leaves, plus more for garnish

Bring a large pot of water to a boil and salt it to taste. While the water is coming to a boil, heat 2 tablespoons of the oil in a large skillet over medium-high heat. Once hot, add the breadcrumbs. Cook, stirring often, until the breadcrumbs are golden and fragrant, 3 to 4 minutes. Transfer the breadcrumbs to a clean plate to cool.

Add the remaining 2 tablespoons oil to the skillet along with the onions and return to medium heat. Season with ¼ teaspoon salt and the pepper. Cook until the onions are soft, about 5 minutes. Add the lemon zest, capers, and sardines and cook, stirring occasionally, until heated through. Remove from the heat.

Once the water comes to a boil, add the pasta and cook until just tender. Drain and reserve ½ cup of the pasta cooking water.

Add the drained pasta to the caper-sardine mixture and toss well over medium heat to combine. Add the ½ cup parsley and the breadcrumbs. If the pasta looks dry and resists tossing, add some of the reserved cooking water to loosen and moisten the dish. Adjust the salt and pepper to taste, if needed. Garnish with additional parsley and serve.

SMOKED SALMON WITH FRIED CAPERS AND SMASHED POTATOES

Serves 4

When I lived in Scotland, *Sainsbury's Magazine* was one of my favorite publications. Each month it offered delicious recipes from the UK's best chefs and recipe writers. All of the recipes were easy to make and tasty. One dish I especially loved was a smashed salmon hash. After misplacing the recipe, I created my own. Pretty pink pieces of warm smoked salmon peek out from under crispy golden potatoes. Mixed with sour cream, capers, and dill, it makes for an impressive weekend brunch or an easy weeknight dinner.

INGREDIENTS

1½ pounds new potatoes, washed and scrubbed

½ teaspoon kosher salt, plus more to taste

2 tablespoons salted butter

2 tablespoons extra-virgin olive oil

3 tablespoons capers, drained and dried

½ teaspoon freshly ground black pepper

2 scallions, trimmed and finely sliced

8 ounces sliced smoked salmon

¼ cup roughly chopped fresh dill

¼ cup sour cream

Fresh sprigs of dill for garnish

Cook the potatoes in a large pot of salted boiling water for 15 to 20 minutes, or until tender when pierced with a fork. Drain well in a colander, then set aside.

In a large skillet over medium-high heat, warm the butter and oil. When the butter has melted and starts to foam, add the capers and fry until crispy, 3 to 4 minutes. Remove the capers from the skillet with a slotted spoon and set aside.

Add the potatoes to the warm skillet and roughly break them up with a wooden spoon. Season with the ½ teaspoon salt and the pepper. Stirring occasionally, cook the potatoes until they are golden brown and crispy at the edges.

Add the scallions, salmon, and chopped dill. Toss to combine and allow the salmon to warm through, 1 to 2 minutes. Turn off the heat and mix in the sour cream. Transfer to a serving bowl or platter. Top with the fried capers and garnish with sprigs of dill. Serve warm.

CAPER AND BUTTER BEAN CHICKEN

Serves 4

Traditional cassoulet is a slow-cooked French casserole full of white beans and different types of meat. Long considered the pinnacle of French home cuisine, it takes both planning and time. This dish is my quick and easy version of cassoulet. A pot of braised chicken thighs, infused with capers, Dijon mustard, and fennel, provides a major hit of flavor to the humble butter bean.

INGREDIENTS

2 pounds bone-in, skin-on chicken thighs and drumsticks
¾ teaspoon kosher salt
¾ teaspoon freshly ground black pepper
3 tablespoons extra-virgin olive oil
2 fennel bulbs, thinly sliced
4 cloves garlic, thinly sliced

1¼ cups chicken stock
Two 15-ounce cans butter beans, rinsed and drained
1 tablespoon red wine or sherry vinegar
2 teaspoons Dijon mustard
1 cup finely chopped flat-leaf parsley leaves
2 tablespoons capers, finely chopped
Fresh fennel fronds for garnish

Season the chicken thighs with the salt and pepper and set aside.

In a large skillet, heat 1 tablespoon of the oil over medium-high heat. Add the thighs to the pan. Brown for 5 minutes on each side and transfer to a large plate.

Add the fennel to the skillet. Scrape up any brown bits in the pan and toss them with the fennel. Cook until the fennel is soft and lightly caramelized, about 5 minutes. Stir in the garlic and cook for 1 minute. Pour in the chicken stock and deglaze the pan. Add the butter beans and stir to combine.

Nestle the chicken thighs on top of the butter beans and pour in any juices that have accumulated on the plate. Cover and cook until the chicken reaches an internal temperature of 165°F, about 20 minutes.

Meanwhile, in a small bowl, whisk the vinegar and mustard with the remaining 2 tablespoons oil. Mix in the parsley and capers. Once the chicken is cooked through, drizzle the herb vinaigrette into the pan. Garnish with fennel fronds and serve in bowls or soup plates.

CHICKPEAS

MENTION CHICKPEAS and most people immediately think of hummus. I, too, adore the creamy blend of chickpeas, lemon juice, tahini, and garlic. It is in my regular rotation of recipes. There is no question that it is a perfect partner for pita bread and fresh vegetables, and it is equally delicious swirled into creamy soups, and spread on toast with mashed avocados and red pepper flakes. However, beyond that velvety puree, there is a world of delicious chickpea recipes.

Whether you call them garbanzo beans, gram, Bengal gram, or Egyptian peas, chickpeas are an extremely versatile legume. From crunchy roasted snacks to savory salads, chickpeas should be a staple in your pantry. Use them to bulk up a soup, create a quick curry, stuff into baked sweet potatoes, garnish a favorite pizza, or whip them into an egg hash.

CANNED VERSUS DRIED

I use canned chickpeas almost exclusively for one simple reason—they are a quick option. There is no question that dried chickpeas are creamier and cheaper than their canned cousin, but they take time to prepare.

Depending on the recipe, dried chickpeas may need to soak for twelve hours or more. For dried chickpeas, there are also two preparation methods to consider: boiled or cold-soaked.

Cold soaking the dried legumes for 24 hours is the traditional technique for making authentic falafel or hummus. Yes, it takes time, but if you want to make the creamiest homemade hummus ever, it is worth the wait.

STORING CHICKPEAS

To store dried, soaked chickpeas, drain all the water and rinse the chickpeas thoroughly. Store them in an airtight container in the refrigerator for up to four days. Dried, soaked chickpeas will last in a sealed freezer-safe container in the freezer for up to six months.

To store dried, boiled chickpeas, drain and rinse, then place them in an airtight container in the refrigerator. They will keep refrigerated in an airtight container for up to three days.

To store canned chickpeas left over after you have opened the can, place them in an airtight container in the refrigerator for up to four days.

WARM ARUGULA, CHORIZO, CHICKPEA, AND CHÈVRE SALAD

Serves 4

When I lived in Glasgow, Scotland, I routinely craved a warm, smoky chorizo salad from Kember & Jones, a fine-food emporium and cafe known for its original culinary creations. And while I still have not replicated this memorable recipe exactly, my version comes pretty close. Be sure to use cured, rather than fresh, chorizo. The garlicky Portuguese version, chouriço, is a great option. If it is not available, Spanish chorizo works as well.

INGREDIENTS

1 tablespoon extra-virgin olive oil

1 pound cured chorizo, cut into ½-inch rounds

1 small red onion, cut into thin half-moons

½ cup oil-packed sundried tomatoes, roughly chopped

One 15.5-ounce can chickpeas, drained and rinsed

½ teaspoon smoked paprika

1 pinch ground cayenne pepper

2 tablespoons chopped fresh thyme leaves

1 tablespoon dry sherry

Kosher salt to taste

Freshly ground black pepper to taste

4 cups arugula, or a mixed herb salad

¼ cup crumbled goat cheese

½ cup Marcona almonds, roughly chopped

Line a plate with paper towels. Warm the oil in a large skillet over medium heat. Add the chorizo and fry until crisp, about 2 minutes per side. Using a slotted spoon, transfer the chorizo to the paper towel–lined plate to drain.

To the same pan add the onion, sundried tomatoes, and chickpeas. Cook, stirring occasionally, until the onions are soft and the chickpeas are crisp, 3 to 5 minutes. Add the paprika, cayenne pepper, and thyme. Stir the in the sherry and return the chorizo to the pan. Heat until warmed through, about 2 minutes. Season to taste with salt and pepper.

Arrange the arugula on a large serving platter. Spoon the chorizo mixture over the arugula and toss. Top the salad with the goat cheese and almonds. Serve warm.

GARLIC CHICKPEA SOUP WITH CILANTRO PESTO

Serves 4

Often the humblest of flavors are the most delicious. Case in point, this simple Portuguese bread soup known as açorda à alentejana. It is rich with garlic, olive oil, and cilantro. For my version, I followed the lead of cookbook author Christopher Kimball and added chickpeas.

INGREDIENTS

Sourdough bread, cut into ¾-inch cubes (3 cups)

¾ cup extra-virgin olive oil

½ cup lightly packed cilantro leaves

½ cup lightly packed flat-leaf parsley leaves

¾ cup grated Parmigiano Reggiano, plus more for serving

2 tablespoons freshly squeezed lemon juice

1 teaspoon sweet paprika

1 teaspoon hot paprika

1 teaspoon kosher salt

½ teaspoon freshly ground black pepper

6 cloves garlic, minced

5 cups chicken stock

Three 15.5-ounce cans chickpeas, drained and rinsed

1 teaspoon white vinegar

4 medium eggs

Freshly ground black pepper to taste

Preheat the oven to 350°F.

In a large bowl, toss the bread with ¼ cup of the olive oil. Place the cubes in a single layer on a parchment-lined baking sheet. Bake for 10 minutes, stirring the bread cubes at about the halfway mark. Continue to bake until golden brown, another 2 to 4 minutes. Set aside.

In a food processor fitted with the metal blade, combine the cilantro, parsley, ¾ cup Parmigiano, lemon juice, both types of paprika, salt, and pepper. Process until the herbs are finely chopped, about 25 seconds. Scrape down the sides and quickly pulse again, if needed. With the machine running, add ¼ cup of the olive oil through the tube and process for another 35 to 45 seconds. Set the pesto aside.

In a stockpot, warm the remaining ¼ cup oil over medium heat. Add the garlic. Cook, stirring constantly, until fragrant, about 1 minute. Be careful not to burn the garlic. Add the stock and the chickpeas. Bring to a gentle simmer over medium-high heat.

Cook, stirring occasionally, until heated through, about 3 minutes. Turn the heat to medium-low and add the pesto. Adjust the salt and pepper if needed.

While the soup is simmering, poach the eggs. Bring 3 to 4 inches of water to a soft boil in a large saucepan. Add the vinegar and reduce the heat to a gentle simmer. Break one egg into a small bowl. Gently slide the egg into the simmering water. Cook until the white is set and the yolk is cooked to your desired doneness, about 4 minutes for a medium egg. Using a slotted spoon, remove the egg and set it aside. Repeat with the remaining eggs.

Divide the bread cubes among four soup bowls. Ladle soup into each bowl and top each serving with a poached egg. Sprinkle with additional Parmigiano and serve warm.

LEMON-PARMESAN CHICKPEA PASTA

Serves 4 to 6

Sumptuous, inexpensive, and easy, this pasta dish epitomizes pantry cooking. The mild flavor of chickpeas makes them an excellent canvas for the lemon, spinach, cream, and Parmesan cheese.

INGREDIENTS

1 teaspoon kosher salt, plus more
  for pasta cooking water
12 ounces bucatini or spaghetti
3 tablespoons grapeseed oil
Two 15.5-ounce cans chickpeas, drained and rinsed
1 tablespoon finely chopped fresh thyme leaves
1 pinch ground cayenne pepper
½ teaspoon freshly ground black pepper

2 tablespoons dry white wine
1 tablespoon freshly squeezed lemon juice
2 shallots, finely chopped
4 cloves garlic, minced
½ cup heavy cream
One 5-ounce bag baby spinach
½ cup finely grated Parmigiano Reggiano

Bring a large pot of water to a boil and salt it to taste. Cook the pasta until it is just short of al dente, about 5 minutes. Turn off the heat. Do not drain the pasta.

In a large skillet, heat the oil over medium-high heat. Add the chickpeas, thyme, and cayenne pepper. Season with the 1 teaspoon salt and the pepper. Cook until the chickpeas start to turn a deep golden brown, 6 to 8 minutes. Using a slotted spoon, transfer the chickpeas to a bowl and set aside.

Reduce the heat to medium and add the wine and lemon juice to deglaze the pan. Add the shallots to the skillet and sauté until they are soft, about 3 minutes. Add the garlic and sauté 1 additional minute.

Pour in the cream and cook until slightly thickened, about 2 minutes. Turn the heat to low and add the spinach a handful at a time. Allow each batch to wilt before adding the next.

Use a slotted spoon or skimmer to transfer the pasta from the pot of water to the pan of spinach and cream sauce. Add the Parmigiano and 1 cup of the pasta cooking water. Stir the mixture briskly over medium-high heat until the sauce is thick, 2 to 3 minutes.

Transfer to a serving platter. Top with the chickpeas. Toss and serve immediately.

COCONUT
MILK

CREAMY CANNED COCONUT MILK is a must-have pantry staple. It adds immense flavor and richness to braised meats, it tempers spicy curries, and it lends body to dark leafy greens.

Coconut milk is made from the shredded flesh of the coconut. The flesh is simmered in water, pureed, and strained to create a rich liquid that lends a lushness to soups, curries, shakes, and so much more. As the simmered liquid sits in the can it naturally separates. The thick milk rises to the top and the thinner liquid remains at the bottom. The solid top layer, known as "coconut cream," provides more fat, taste, and protein. By vigorously shaking the can, you can incorporate the dispersed milk. Alternatively, you can empty the entire can into your recipe and it will come together during the cooking process.

STORING UNUSED COCONUT MILK

The contents of an open can of coconut milk will last up to one week in the refrigerator and up to one month in the freezer. To store, pour any leftover milk into a refrigerator- or freezer-safe container with a tight-fitting lid. If freezing, leave at least ½-inch head space, as the coconut milk will expand. To use frozen coconut milk, defrost it, then blend it with an immersion blender for 30 seconds to emulsify.

USES FOR COCONUT MILK

Pureed soups: Coconut milk can be used in place of dairy cream or milk in any recipe that calls for them. It adds a mild flavor and sweet undertone. Try it in a silky zucchini soup, carrot-ginger soup, creamy curried cauliflower soup, or a winter root vegetable soup with pears.

Curries: Curry is simply a dish that includes meat or vegetables cooked in a heavily spiced sauce. With regional variations throughout the world, there are many different styles and flavors. Many curries are enhanced by the addition of coconut milk.

Breakfast: Substitute coconut milk for dairy milk in your oatmeal, pancakes, or waffles. It is also delicious blended into smoothies.

COCONUT PANCAKES

Makes 6 to 8 pancakes

Coconut pancakes, known as kanom krok in Thailand, are a wildly popular street food. Made in cast-iron pans with round indentations, each takes the form of a little pod—a crispy cake with a soft, warm custard interior. Though kanom krok are vastly different from the thick and fluffy pancakes of North America, this recipe is very much inspired by Thai flavors.

INGREDIENTS

2 cups whole-wheat flour

¼ cup sugar

1 tablespoon plus 1 teaspoon baking powder

¼ teaspoon baking soda

½ teaspoon sea salt

1½ cups (from one 13.5 ounce can) coconut milk

1 large egg

3 tablespoons coconut or vegetable oil, plus more for frying

2 teaspoons pure vanilla extract

Honey and shredded coconut for serving

In a large mixing bowl, whisk together the flour, sugar, baking powder, baking soda, and salt. Add the coconut milk, egg, coconut oil, and vanilla. Mix to combine.

Place a large skillet or griddle over medium heat. When a few drops of water sizzle on the surface, add a thin layer of coconut oil. For each pancake, spoon ¼ cup of batter onto the skillet or griddle, working in batches.

Cook until bubbles form on the top, 2 to 3 minutes. Carefully flip the pancakes and cook until golden brown, another 2 minutes. Transfer to a platter, cover loosely with aluminum foil, and keep warm in the oven. Continue until you have used up the remaining batter, brushing the cooking surface with more oil as needed. Serve with honey and shredded coconut.

COCONUT-BRAISED GREENS

Serves 4

Pairing hardy leafy greens with creamy coconut milk, hot chile, ginger, and spices gives them incredible flavor. Toasted coconut adds a nutty, crunchy touch.

INGREDIENTS

½ cup unsweetened coconut flakes

4 bunches mixed hardy greens, such as Tuscan kale,
  Swiss chard, and mustard greens

¼ cup coconut oil

4 cloves garlic, minced

3 large shallots, finely chopped

I small red Thai chile, thinly sliced

One I-inch piece ginger, peeled and thinly sliced

I teaspoon kosher salt, plus more to taste

I tablespoon mustard seeds, toasted

½ teaspoon ground coriander

¼ teaspoon ground turmeric

I cup coconut milk

Freshly ground black pepper to taste

Preheat the oven to 350°F.

Spread the coconut flakes on a parchment-lined baking sheet and toast until a few turn golden brown and some remain white, 4 to 6 minutes. Remove from the oven, set aside, and allow to cool.

Remove the stalks from the greens and discard. Roughly chop the leaves and set aside.

Heat the oil in a large skillet over medium heat. Add the garlic and shallots and sauté, stirring often, for 2 minutes. Add the chile, ginger, 1 teaspoon salt, mustard seeds, coriander, and turmeric. Stir to distribute the spices evenly and cook until fragrant, about 1 minute.

Add the coconut milk to the skillet and bring to a simmer. Add the greens, a handful at a time, allowing each batch to wilt slightly before adding the next. Cook, tossing occasionally, until the greens are tender and the mixture is creamy, about 15 minutes. Season with more salt and pepper, if needed.

Transfer the greens to a platter. Top with the coconut flakes and serve warm.

COCONUT MILK–STEAMED MUSSELS WITH LEMONGRASS

Serves 2

My mussel consumption fell drastically after moving from Scotland. What had once been on my weekly dinner rotation—mussels bathed in wine with a few herbs—began to appear on the menu only a few times a year. But leave it to the brilliant cookbook author Melissa Clark to take mussels in a new direction and place them back on my recipe radar by pairing them with coconut milk, inspiring me to create this delicious dish.

INGREDIENTS

2 tablespoons coconut oil

3 shallots, finely diced

4 cloves garlic, minced

2 stalks lemongrass, outer layers removed, very finely chopped

1 serrano chile pepper, seeded and finely chopped

1½ cups (from one 13.5 ounce can) coconut milk

½ cup dry white wine

2 pounds fresh mussels, cleaned and beards removed

1 tablespoon freshly squeezed lemon juice, plus more to taste

1 teaspoon freshly squeezed lime juice

1 teaspoon Thai fish sauce

¼ cup finely chopped cilantro leaves

¼ cup finely chopped flat-leaf parsley leaves

Crusty bread for dipping

In a large pot, heat the oil over medium until hot. Add the shallots, garlic, lemongrass, and serrano. Cook until soft, about 3 minutes. Add the coconut milk, wine, and mussels. Cover with a tight-fitting lid and cook until the mussels have opened, 5 to 7 minutes. Discard any mussels that do not open.

Remove the pot from the heat and use a slotted spoon to transfer the mussels to a large bowl, leaving the liquid in the pot. Stir the 1 tablespoon lemon juice, lime juice, fish sauce, cilantro, and parsley into the liquid. Taste and add more lemon juice, if needed.

Place the mussels in two large shallow bowls. Ladle the broth over the mussels and serve them with bread.

COUSCOUS

I REMEMBER READING a *New York Times* article about couscous written in 1992 by food writer Florence Fabricant. In it she enthused over couscous and declared the North African pasta a rising star in American kitchens, on supermarket shelves, and on restaurant menus. She went on to describe boiling couscous in a savory broth with butter and fluffing it with a fork. Intrigued, I went on a search for the semolina-based cousin to pasta, but I came up empty-handed.

A few years later I came across a *Bon Appétit* recipe featuring couscous. The dish was scented with ginger, turmeric, cinnamon, and saffron and punctuated with raisins, chickpeas, and acorn squash. I knew that I needed to search again for couscous. That time I scored a box at my local supermarket. The dish was flavorful and easy, yet couscous seemed exotic at the time. Now that couscous is widely available, it has become an essential staple in my pantry.

Long a standard in the cuisines of North African countries, among them, Libya, Morocco, Tunisia, and Algeria, it also plays a large role in Middle Eastern dishes. Couscous marries well with fruit, vegetables, meat, seafood, and poultry.

TYPES OF COUSCOUS

The three basic types of couscous are Moroccan, Israeli, and Lebanese. Moroccan and Israeli are the two most commonly found in American markets.

Moroccan couscous: The smallest of the varieties, a piece of this tiny Moroccan pasta is about three times the size of a grain of cornmeal. Moroccan couscous is made by mixing ground semolina with water and rolling the dough into granules. The granules are then steamed and dried. Due to its small size, it cooks very quickly.

Israeli couscous: A piece of Israeli couscous, also called pearl couscous, is about the size of a peppercorn. Toasted rather than dried, Israeli couscous has a nuttier flavor than Moroccan and a soft yet chewy bite. It is wonderful as a base for cold salads and can be cooked risotto-style.

Lebanese couscous: Lebanese couscous is also known as moghrabieh pearls. This type of couscous is the largest of the three varieties, with each piece about the size of a small pea. It features in a traditional Lebanese stew that consists of couscous, chicken, chickpeas, onions, and spices.

STORING COUSCOUS

Couscous should be stored in a well-sealed box or container and placed in a cool, dark pantry. Stored properly it can last up to two years.

Cooked couscous will last about three days in the refrigerator in a tightly sealed container. To reheat, add 1 to 3 tablespoons water for each cup of leftover couscous. Reheat in a saucepan over medium-low heat.

CLEMENTINE AND PISTACHIO COUSCOUS BREAKFAST BOWLS

Serves 4 as breakfast

Much like steel-cut oatmeal or wheat germ, couscous makes a satisfying breakfast. Couscous is very versatile and its flavor and texture distinguish it from standard breakfast fare.

INGREDIENTS

½ cup pistachios

1¼ cups Moroccan couscous

¼ teaspoon ground cinnamon

Finely grated zest and juice of 1 navel orange

1 teaspoon butter

2 tablespoons honey, plus more for drizzling

4 clementines, peeled, seeded, and separated into sections

1 cup raspberries

2 tablespoons plain Greek yogurt

Preheat the oven to 375°F. Spread the nuts in a single layer on a baking sheet and toast until lightly golden, 3 to 4 minutes. Let the nuts rest until cool enough to handle, then chop and set aside.

Place the couscous and the cinnamon in a large heatproof bowl and set aside.

In a medium saucepan, combine the orange zest and juice, butter, 2 tablespoons honey, and 1½ cups water. Bring to a boil. Pour the boiling liquid over the bowl of couscous.

Tightly cover the bowl with plastic wrap and set aside at room temperature for 10 minutes to absorb the liquid. Fluff the couscous with a fork and mix in the pistachios.

Divide the couscous evenly among four bowls. Top each couscous-filled bowl with clementine sections and ¼ cup raspberries. Add yogurt and a drizzle of honey to each and serve.

CREAMY COUSCOUS AND CHICKPEA GRATIN

Serves 4 as a light main course

With a glass of red wine, this vegetarian main course can serve as a wonderful and warming weekend lunch, or a delightful side dish. It was inspired by Nigel Slater's chickpea and spinach gratin. I swapped roasted garlic and tomatoes for the spinach and added pearl couscous. Scented with rosemary and topped with feta, it is a family favorite.

INGREDIENTS

2 cups yellow and red grape tomatoes

4 cloves garlic

2 tablespoons extra-virgin olive oil, plus more for drizzling

1 tablespoon white balsamic vinegar

1 teaspoon kosher salt

½ teaspoon freshly ground black pepper

2 sprigs fresh rosemary

2 cups vegetable stock

1 teaspoon freshly squeezed lemon juice

1 teaspoon ground cumin

1½ cups Israeli couscous

One 15-ounce can chickpeas, drained and rinsed

¼ cup sliced scallions, white and pale green parts only

1 cup crumbled feta

⅓ cup grated Parmigiano Reggiano

Fresh tyme for garnish

Preheat the oven to 425°F.

In a medium bowl, toss the tomatoes and garlic with the 2 tablespoons oil, vinegar, salt, and pepper. Transfer to a 9-inch square baking dish or gratin dish. Top with the rosemary sprigs. Roast until the tomatoes are soft, about 20 minutes.

In a medium saucepan, bring the stock to a simmer over medium-high heat. Stir in the lemon juice and cumin. Set aside.

Once the tomatoes are roasted, remove them from the oven and discard the rosemary. Fold in the couscous, chickpeas, scallions, and the stock mixture. Cover the pan tightly with foil and return it to the oven for an additional 20 minutes. The couscous should be al dente.

When the couscous is just cooked through, remove the foil and fold in the feta. Sprinkle on the Parmigiano and bake, uncovered, until the feta melts, about 5 minutes. Drizzle with oil, garnish with thyme, and serve.

SICILIAN-INSPIRED COUSCOUS WITH CALAMARI

Serves 4 as a light main course

I will never forget the first time I had this lusty, lovely dish at Babbo in New York City. While it was years ago, I can still remember the zesty flavors, soft squid, chewy couscous, crisp pine nuts, and salty caperberries. Not only is my version quick and easy to prepare, but it will also impress any guest without denting your budget.

INGREDIENTS

1 tablespoon kosher salt

1 cup Israeli couscous

3 tablespoons extra-virgin olive oil, plus more for drizzling

2 cloves garlic, thinly sliced

2 tablespoons pine nuts

1 tablespoon dried currants

1 tablespoon raisins

1 teaspoon red pepper flakes

¼ cup caperberries

1 cup canned coarsely chopped tomatoes and their juices, preferably Mutti

¼ cup dry white wine

3 tablespoons basil pesto, preferably Seggiano

1½ pounds calamari bodies, sliced into ½-inch rings

3 scallions, white and pale green parts thinly sliced

Freshly ground black pepper to taste

Bring 3 quarts of water to a boil. Add the salt and the couscous. Cook the couscous in the boiling water for 2 minutes. Drain, then immediately rinse under cold running water to stop the cooking. Set aside to drain again.

In a large skillet, heat the 3 tablespoons olive oil over medium-high heat. Add the garlic, pine nuts, currants, raisins, and red pepper flakes. Sauté until the nuts are just golden brown, about 2 minutes. Add the caperberries, tomatoes, wine, pesto, and couscous, and bring to a boil over high heat.

Add the calamari and scallions and reduce the heat to medium. Stir to combine and simmer for 2 to 3 minutes, or until the calamari is just cooked and completely opaque. Season to taste with pepper and adjust the salt, if necessary. To serve, divide among small plates. Drizzle with olive oil and serve immediately.

DILL

THE OMNIPRESENCE OF DILL IN RUSSIAN CUISINE is legendary. From Olivier salad (Russian potato salad) to sturgeon caviar drizzled with dill oil and warm bowls of borscht, it permeates the culinary culture of the country. I once read that Russians eat enough dill each year to fill a large suitcase. My love of dill is well known to my family and friends. Fresh, air-dried, freeze-dried, seeds—I love it all. Perhaps I was Russian in a past life.

While dill is native to southwest Asia and, as noted, wildly popular in Russia, it is also widely used in Mediterranean and Scandinavian countries. Although famous in the United States mostly for giving pickles their kick and infusing ranch dressing, this herb offers so much more. In my humble opinion, it is one of the most fragrant and flavorful herbs in the kitchen.

GETTING THE MOST FROM DILL

Given the choice, I go with fresh dill, yet that is not always an option. I find that frozen dill holds its flavor much better than dried dill, and for that reason I keep Litehouse freeze-dried dill in my pantry year-round. You can also easily freeze a batch of your own.

TWO METHODS FOR FREEZING DILL:

Dill ice cubes: Place the desired amount of dill leaves in a blender or food processor. Pulse to finely chop the leaves. Add a few drops of water and pulse until the chopped leaves form a paste; add more water as needed. Spoon the dill paste into an ice cube tray and freeze. Once frozen, transfer the cubes to a resealable plastic bag and store in the freezer. A dill ice cube will add a burst of fresh flavor to any dish. There is a one-to-one correspondence between the frozen and fresh sprigs. Also, one ice cube of dill is roughly 1 tablespoon.

Frozen dill sprigs: Wash fresh dill in cold water, then pat it dry with a paper towel. Lay the sprigs on a baking sheet in a single layer. Place the baking sheet in the freezer to flash freeze. Once the dill sprigs are frozen, transfer them to a freezer bag and return them to the freezer. When ready to use, pull out the same number of the frozen dill sprigs you would need if you were using fresh dill. However, since the flavor of frozen dill starts to fade after six months, you may need to add an extra sprig to your dish for full flavor if your dill has been in the freezer for a long time. After a full year, you should harvest and freeze a new batch.

Note that dill loses its flavor as it is cooked. Add it at the last minute to preserve the taste.

PAIRING DILL

Foods that pair well with dill include:

asparagus	eggs	salmon
avocados	fish	sour cream
beets	lamb	tomatoes
cabbage	lemon	white sauces
carrots	onion	yogurt
celery	potatoes	zucchini
cream cheese	pumpkin	
cucumber	rice	

Herbs and spices that go well with dill include:

basil	mint
cumin	parsley
garlic	turmeric
ginger	

CHILLED DILL-CUCUMBER AND AVOCADO SOUP

Serves 2 as a main course or 4 as a starter

An impromptu lunch by the pool with a friend sent me in search of a quick and cold soup. I turned to a favorite *New York Times* recipe but realized I was missing a few herbs and some fresh ingredients. So I adapted the soup with ingredients from my pantry and vegetables I had on hand. Cucumbers and avocados spun together in the blender make for an instant meal, and the humble cucumber takes on renewed flavor when combined with fresh dill. For dinner, top the soup with crabmeat or a lobster tail.

INGREDIENTS

1 pound cucumbers, peeled, seeded, and chopped

2 cups buttermilk

2 large cloves garlic, smashed and roughly chopped

3 anchovy filets, rinsed and drained

1½ teaspoons hot sauce, preferably Tabasco

⅓ cup loosely packed fresh dill, plus more for garnish

1 teaspoon white wine vinegar

1 teaspoon kosher or sea salt

2 small ripe avocados, pitted, peeled, and chopped

Freshly squeezed juice of 1 lemon

In the bowl of a food processor fitted with the metal blade or in a blender, combine the cucumbers, buttermilk, garlic, anchovies, hot sauce, ⅓ cup dill, vinegar, salt, avocados, and lemon juice. Pulse or blend until smooth. Taste and adjust the seasoning as needed.

Chill the soup, covered, in the refrigerator until it is cold. Garnish with fresh dill and serve.

ESPRESSO POWDER

MORE OFTEN THAN NOT, the difference between a good dish and a great dish comes down to a single ingredient. One ingredient that I reach for over and over again is instant espresso powder. Dark and mysterious, with a slight smoky note, it is a pantry item untapped by many that adds depth and complexity to recipes ranging from chocolate mousse to braised meats and vinaigrettes. However, do not let the name fool you. Espresso powder does not add coffee flavor to food but intensifies the taste, much as a pinch of salt takes flavors from flat to robust.

There's no question that espresso powder boosts the flavor of cookies, tarts, cakes, and brownies, and makes chocolate desserts taste even richer. But as someone who loves savory dishes, I find espresso powder also amps up the flavors of cayenne, cinnamon, cumin, chili powder, and paprika. I often add it to a pot of chili, a lush beef stew, or a mole sauce.

WHAT IS ESPRESSO POWDER?

Espresso powder is made from darkly roasted coffee beans that have been ground, brewed, dried, and then ground into a very fine powder.

TIPS FOR USING ESPRESSO POWDER

Espresso powder is much more concentrated than instant coffee, so a small amount goes a long way. Too much espresso powder will cause baked goods to taste bitter.

Espresso complements a whole host of flavors, including caramel, gingerbread, dark berries, sea salt, and cheeses.

Like flaky sea salt, espresso powder can be used as a finishing component on desserts. Try sprinkling a pinch on a few scoops of chocolate or vanilla ice cream.

Add a few teaspoons to barbecue sauce to amp up the flavor.

ESPRESSO POWDER VERSUS INSTANT COFFEE

Technically, an espresso bean is a coffee bean, but espresso powder (sometimes labeled instant espresso or instant espresso powder) and instant coffee powder are quite different. Espresso powder delivers a much darker flavor than instant coffee. Using instant coffee for baking will not add the same rich notes as using espresso powder. Doubling up on instant coffee (in lieu of espresso powder) to add bolder flavor to food still will not produce the same results and may impart a bitter taste.

MAKE YOUR OWN

Preheat the oven to 170°F. Spread used coffee grounds on a parchment-lined baking sheet. Bake until the grounds are dry and slightly crunchy, 2 to 3 hours. Transfer the roasted grounds to a coffee grinder. Process to a very fine powder. Store in an airtight container for up to five months.

ESPRESSO LENTIL BROWNIES

Makes 20 brownies

I first learned of lentil brownies while watching Joy Bauer make them on the *Today* show. I scribbled down notes and played with her recipe. The result is delicious, chewy brownies that are easy to prepare and high in protein. Thanks to espresso powder, chocolate, and cocoa powder, they are also high in flavor.

INGREDIENTS

Nonstick cooking spray
  for coating the baking dish

¼ cup walnut oil

¼ cup applesauce

½ cup unsweetened cocoa powder

½ cup cooked red lentils

½ cup semisweet
  chocolate chips

3 large eggs

2 tablespoons espresso powder

½ teaspoon ground cinnamon

I tablespoon vanilla extract

¾ cup maple syrup

¾ cup unbleached
  all-purpose flour

1½ teaspoons baking powder

½ teaspoon kosher salt

Preheat the oven to 350°F. Coat a 9½ by 11-inch baking pan with nonstick cooking spray and set aside.

In a food processor fitted with the metal blade, blend the walnut oil, applesauce, cocoa powder, and lentils until smooth.

Melt the chocolate chips in a small saucepan over low heat. Add them to the lentil mixture in the food processor. Pulse a few times to combine. Set aside and allow to cool until warm but not hot.

Whisk together the eggs, espresso powder, cinnamon, vanilla, and maple syrup in a large bowl. Stir in the warm chocolate-lentil mixture until combined.

In a separate bowl, combine the flour, baking powder, and salt. Add the dry ingredients to the wet ingredients in 3 to 4 additions, stirring to combine between additions. Give the mixture one last stir from the bottom with a spatula to be sure everything is incorporated and no dry ingredients remain at the bottom. Pour the batter into the prepared pan. Bake until the brownies are firm in the center and a toothpick inserted comes out clean, 20 to 30 minutes. Allow to cool completely before cutting into 20 squares.

FARRO

FARRO IS A DELECTABLE ANCIENT GRAIN and a staple in Italian cooking. Generally grown in the regions of Lazio, Tuscany, the Marches, and Umbria, it is appreciated for its distinct nutty flavor and chewy texture. Toasting this grain in a dry skillet before cooking it creates an even nuttier taste.

Throughout Tuscany, farro is widely used in soups. Minestra di farro, a simple soup made with onions, pancetta, olive oil, potatoes, and farro, is a regional favorite. In the walled town of Lucca, farro and bean soup is an institution at Trattoria da Leo. And in Umbria, a savory soup of tomatoes, broad beans, porcini mushrooms, beef stock, and farro is typical of the region's country cooking.

Like Arborio rice, farro releases starch when cooked, creating a creamy, binding liquid. Unlike rice, however, farro does not take on a porridge-like consistency; instead, it remains tender and retains its distinct bite.

Less filling than brown rice, with undertones of oats and barley, farro complements a variety of dishes. Dressed with a lemony vinaigrette, it makes a lovely salad. Swap it for oatmeal and enjoy a warm bowl of farro with a dollop of yogurt, nuts, and fresh or oven-roasted fruit. Keep a batch of cooked farro in the refrigerator for easy lunches. Or serve it as a base for a satisfying grain bowl, with cooked vegetables and a favorite protein, at dinnertime.

TYPES OF FARRO

These are the three most common types of farro, though in the United States you will rarely find anything but pearled farro:

Whole farro contains the entire husk and bran. While it is the most nutritious form, it also requires at least 40 minutes of cooking time.

Semi-pearled farro has no husk and only a portion of the bran. Milder in flavor, it takes 25 to 30 minutes to cook.

Pearled farro is by far the type most commonly available in grocery stores. With no husk or bran, it requires only about 15 minutes to cook.

TO RINSE OR NOT TO RINSE

As the result of processing, farro is sometimes covered in a dusty residue. To remove the powdery coating, or any debris, rinse the farro in a fine-mesh strainer under cool running water before cooking.

STORAGE

Store uncooked pearled farro in the pantry for up to six months and in the freezer for up to one year. Once the package is opened, store the unused portion in an airtight container away from moisture and light. Cooked farro can be refrigerated for up to three days.

FARRO BREAKFAST BOWLS WITH CINNAMON APPLES

Serves 4 as breakfast

Composed of sautéed apples with a sprinkling of cinnamon, dried cranberries, and farro, this breakfast bowl is delicious either warm or cold and can also be enhanced with a splash of oat milk. Or you could do as my husband does and spoon it over vanilla ice cream.

INGREDIENTS

½ cup pearled farro

¼ teaspoon kosher salt

1 tablespoon coconut oil

1 gala, Fuji, or Granny Smith apple, cored and cubed

¼ teaspoon ground cinnamon

¼ cup roughly chopped toasted hazelnuts

¼ cup dried cranberries

½ cup plain Greek yogurt

¼ cup honey

Combine the farro, salt, and 1½ cups water in a medium saucepan. Place the pan over medium-high heat and bring to a boil. Lower the heat to a simmer. Cover the pan with a tight-fitting lid and cook until the farro is plump and tender, 15 to 20 minutes. Drain the farro in a fine-mesh sieve to remove any remaining water and set aside.

In a small skillet warm the oil over medium-high heat. Add the apples and sauté them until soft and golden, about 5 minutes. Add the cinnamon and stir to combine. Fold in the hazelnuts and cranberries.

Divide the farro among four bowls and top each portion with the apple mixture. Add a dollop of yogurt and a drizzle of honey to each and serve.

WATERMELON AND FARRO SALAD

Serves 4 as a side dish or light main course

This refreshing summertime salad was inspired by my friend Tricia Foley. For my book *Entertaining at Home*, she created a lovely salad of heirloom cherry tomatoes and ripe peaches. I added farro and swapped watermelon for the peaches. Toasting the farro before cooking it adds a layer of rich nuttiness.

INGREDIENTS

I cup pearled farro

1¼ teaspoons kosher salt

2 cups cubed seedless watermelon

2 cups halved yellow cherry tomatoes

¼ cup chopped fresh mint

½ cup chopped fresh basil

2 tablespoons extra-virgin olive oil

I tablespoon sherry vinegar

2 tablespoons finely chopped shallot

I tablespoon freshly squeezed lemon juice

½ teaspoon freshly ground black pepper

⅓ cup crumbled feta cheese

Fresh mint sprigs for garnish

Preheat the oven to 375°F.

Spread the farro on a rimmed baking sheet in a single layer and bake until lightly toasted and fragrant, about 10 minutes.

Combine 2 cups water, the farro, and ¼ teaspoon of the salt in a medium saucepan and bring to a boil. Cover, reduce the heat to low, and simmer for 20 minutes. Drain the farro in a fine-mesh sieve to remove any remaining water. Set aside and cool to room temperature.

In a salad bowl combine the watermelon, tomatoes, mint, and basil. Add the farro and toss.

In a small bowl whisk the oil, vinegar, shallot, lemon juice, remaining 1 teaspoon salt, and pepper. Pour the vinaigrette over the salad and toss to combine. Top with feta and fresh mint, and serve.

TOASTED FARRO PESTO SALAD

Serves 4 as a side dish or light main course

Cherry tomatoes paired with spinach pesto, artichoke hearts, and nutty toasted farro is a simply delicious combination.

INGREDIENTS

2 cups pearled farro

3½ cups vegetable stock or water

1½ cups baby spinach

1 tablespoon basil pesto, preferably Seggiano

⅓ cup salted toasted sunflower seeds

½ cup grated Parmigiano Reggiano

4 cloves garlic, minced

1 teaspoon kosher salt

1 teaspoon freshly ground black pepper

3 tablespoons extra-virgin olive oil

½ cup plain Greek yogurt

1 cup halved cherry tomatoes

2 cups jarred artichoke hearts in oil, drained and quartered

One 5-ounce package baby arugula

¼ cup finely shredded Parmigiano Reggiano

Preheat the oven to 350°F.

Spread the farro on a rimmed baking sheet in a single layer. Bake until brown and fragrant, about 10 minutes. Remove from the oven and set aside.

In a large saucepan, bring the vegetable stock or water to a boil. Add the farro and stir to combine. Reduce the heat to medium-low and simmer, uncovered, until the farro is tender with a slight chew, about 25 minutes. If all the liquid is absorbed before the farro is tender, add water in small amounts as needed. Drain the farro in a fine-mesh sieve to remove any remaining water. Spread the farro in a single layer on a parchment paper–lined baking sheet to cool for about 20 minutes.

Place the spinach, pesto, sunflower seeds, grated Parmigiano, garlic, salt, and pepper in the bowl of a food processor fitted with the metal blade. Pulse 15 to 20 times, scraping down the sides of the bowl as needed. With the food processor running, add the oil through the tube in a thin stream, and process until it is incorporated. Add the yogurt and pulse to combine. Transfer to a large bowl.

Transfer the cooled farro to the bowl and toss with the dressing. Gently fold in the tomatoes and artichoke hearts. Divide the arugula among four serving plates. Top with the farro mixture and shredded cheese.

LEMON-CHICKEN FARRO SOUP

Serves 4 to 6 as a main course

This amazing soup was inspired by Colu Henry, one of my favorite food writers and recipe developers. Using toasted farro in place of noodles makes this delicious dish heartier. Fresh lemon juice and zest add a lovely flavor.

INGREDIENTS

2 tablespoons extra-virgin olive oil

1 pound boneless, skinless chicken thighs

1 teaspoon kosher salt, plus more to taste

½ teaspoon freshly ground black pepper, plus more to taste

2 leeks, white and pale green parts thinly sliced

2 shallots, finely diced

3 medium carrots, thinly sliced into rounds

3 ribs celery, thinly sliced

4 cloves garlic, finely chopped

½ teaspoon red pepper flakes

1 tablespoon chopped fresh thyme leaves

1 tablespoon chopped fresh rosemary leaves

1 cup pearled farro

6 cups chicken broth

¼ cup freshly squeezed lemon juice

5 cups roughly chopped spinach

Grated lemon zest to taste

Heat 1 tablespoon of the oil in a large stockpot or Dutch oven over medium-high heat. Season the chicken to taste with salt and pepper. Brown the thighs on each side, about 3 to 5 minutes per side. Remove from the pot and set aside.

Add the remaining 1 tablespoon oil to the pot. Add the leeks, shallots, carrots, and celery. Cook, stirring occasionally, until the vegetables soften and start to brown, 4 to 6 minutes. Add the garlic, red pepper flakes, thyme, and rosemary, and cook until fragrant, about 1 additional minute. Mix in the 1 teaspoon salt and ½ teaspoon black pepper.

Add the farro and cook, stirring frequently, until lightly toasted, 1 to 2 minutes. Add the broth and the chicken thighs. Bring to a boil, then reduce the heat to a simmer. Cook until the chicken has cooked through and is no longer pink, about 10 minutes.

With a slotted spoon, remove the chicken and transfer it to a cutting board. When cool enough to handle, shred the chicken. Meanwhile, continue to simmer the soup until the farro is tender, about 20 minutes. Return the chicken to the pot and stir in the spinach. Allow the spinach to wilt.

Taste and adjust the seasoning. Ladle the soup into bowls and top with lemon zest.

G

GHEE

I EXPERIENCED SO MANY DIFFERENT FOODS and cooking techniques while I was living in Scotland. One of the benefits of residing in a brownstone was enjoying the amazing aromas that wafted down the hallway and up the stairs at dinnertime. My downstairs neighbor was the queen of the kitchen and always eager to share both meals and recipes. From preserved lemons with lamb cooked in a traditional tagine pot to Bombay potatoes simmered on her Aga stove, she could prepare a feast.

My neighbor also taught me the virtues of cooking with gorgeous golden ghee. With a nutty smell, clean taste, and a flavor more decadent than butter, it had me hooked instantly. Slathered over a whole roasted chicken, tossed with crispy new potatoes, or used to sauté parsnips and herbs, ghee was a game-changer. Though it was once hard to find in American grocery stores, there are now dozens of brands available. And while ghee seems to be having a moment, it has been used in cooking throughout the Indian subcontinent and the Middle East for thousands of years.

WHAT IS GHEE?

While ghee is a type of clarified butter, it does differ from its French counterpart. Unlike French clarified butter, which is cooked until the water evaporates and the milk solids separate, ghee is cooked until the milk solids begin to caramelize, creating a toasty taste and aroma.

A HIGH SMOKE POINT

With the milk solids removed, ghee can be cooked to a much higher temperature, 485°F versus 350°F for butter, making it ideal for sautéing, frying, or roasting without the fat burning and smoking.

A LONGER SHELF LIFE

In the absence of milk solids, ghee can be stored unopened in a cool, dark pantry for up to one year. Once opened, it can be kept unrefrigerated for up to three months and in the refrigerator for up to one year.

USES FOR GHEE

Spread it on toast, pour it over popcorn, sauté with garlic and ginger, or blend it into your coffee for a mid-morning energy boost.

BOMBAY POTATOES

Serves 4

I first tried Bombay potatoes, sometimes called Bombay aloo, at Mother India's Cafe, situated across from the Kelvingrove Art Gallery in the west end of Glasgow. The spicy baby potatoes, simmered in aromatic spices, were simply divine. It is an easy-to-prepare dish that is perfect to serve as an appetizer or a side. Be sure to use a waxy potato, such as new potatoes, red bliss, or fingerlings, which are low in starch, high in moisture, and have a creamier, firmer flesh. I prefer not to peel potatoes in order to protect their structure.

INGREDIENTS

½ teaspoon kosher salt, plus more for boiling water

1 pound waxy baby potatoes, unpeeled

2 tablespoons ghee

1 teaspoon cumin seeds

½ teaspoon brown mustard seeds

1 teaspoon ground coriander

1 teaspoon ground cumin

½ teaspoon ground turmeric

½ teaspoon Aleppo pepper or red pepper flakes

Freshly squeezed juice of 1 lime

½ teaspoon garam masala

1 tablespoon freeze-dried parsley flakes

Bring a large pot of salted water to a gentle boil. Add the potatoes and cook until tender, 12 to 15 minutes, making sure not to overcook them. Drain and set aside.

In a large skillet heat the ghee. Once the ghee has melted, add the cumin and mustard seeds. Reduce the heat to medium-low and add the ½ teaspoon salt and spices. Sauté for 30 seconds. Add 3 tablespoons water and the boiled potatoes. Mix, allowing the spices to coat the potatoes. Cover and cook until the water evaporates and the spices adhere to the potatoes, about 5 minutes.

Transfer the potatoes to a serving dish. Top with the lime juice, garam masala, and parsley, and serve.

HONEY

THICK, GOLDEN, CREAMY, AND FRAGRANT, honey is as old as written history. In ancient Georgia it was buried with the dead to be carried into the afterlife, while in ancient Egypt bees were kept in the temples to produce honey for mummification, sweetening food, and medicinal uses.

From a small drizzle on a piece of toast smothered with soft cheese to the creation of a sweet and peppery vinaigrette, honey is one of my go-to pantry ingredients. Next to my Merula extra-virgin olive oil, fleur de sel, and PepperMate peppermill, you will always find a jar of honey from our neighborhood farmer's market. Local honey is a good bet, as it contains a blend of regional pollen, which can help to strengthen the immune system and reduce pollen allergies. Note that honey should not be fed to babies under one year of age.

While more than 300 varieties of honey are available in the United States alone, there are three basic categories:

SINGLE-ORIGIN: When bees are allowed to access only one type of flower, a single-origin honey (also referred to as single-source or monofloral) is produced. Clover honey, the most popular variety in the United States, is made from nectar collected solely from clover flowers.

MULTIFLORAL: Often called wildflower honey or millefiori ("one thousand flowers") in Italy, this is the most common type of local honey. Because this honey is made from flowers that bloom at indeterminate times, its flavor and its scent can differ from year to year.

LOCAL: Nectar that is collected from a specific region or territory is referred to as local honey. While there is no set standard that defines the term local, it is generally agreed to refer to honey produced within a certain radius from your home, ranging from five miles to one hundred, and the nearer the better.

A FEW HONEYS THAT ARE FUN TO TRY
Orange blossom honey possesses a lovely citrus grove fragrance. The color of pale amber and bursting with orange notes, it is delicious paired with brie or Camembert.

Avocado honey is dark amber in color with a thick consistency similar to that of molasses. While it does come from the nectar of avocado trees, it does not taste like the fruit.

Eucalyptus honey has a mild sweetness and a strong earthy flavor. With undertones of menthol and caramel, it is perfect for stirring into tea.

HOW TO TASTE HONEY
The best way to learn to distinguish between different types of honey is to taste them in side-by-side comparisons. Spoon a small amount of honey from the jar, taking in the aroma. Then allow the honey to melt on the front of your tongue. As it melts, a nuanced flavor is tasted. Eating an unsalted cracker and taking a sip of room-temperature water between each tasting will help to neutralize your palate.

HONEY DATES AND BLUE CHEESE

Serves 4 to 6 as a starter

Serve this simple appetizer with a wedge of good blue cheese, water crackers, and a crisp rosé or ruby port wine for a memorable starter.

INGREDIENTS

16 medjool dates

¼ cup Marcona almonds, coarsely chopped

¼ cup honey

2 ounces Gorgonzola, crumbled

One 8-ounce wedge good blue cheese, such as Stilton, Maytag, or Danish

Sprig of fresh thyme for garnish

One 4¼-ounce box water crackers

Using a sharp paring knife, cut a slit in each date to remove the pit, leaving the dates whole. Arrange the pitted dates on a serving platter. Sprinkle the chopped almonds over them and drizzle with the honey. Top with the crumbled Gorgonzola. Place the wedge of blue cheese on the platter. Garnish with thyme and serve with the crackers.

TOAST WITH HONEY AND PROSCIUTTO

Serves 2 as a light main course

Toasted sourdough bread topped with creamy tart goat cheese, salty prosciutto, sweet honey, and fresh thyme is a simply sublime meal.

INGREDIENTS

2 slices sourdough bread

1 tablespoon extra-virgin olive oil

2 tablespoons honey

1 tablespoon minced fresh thyme

2 teaspoons finely grated lemon zest

¼ cup soft goat cheese

4 thin slices prosciutto

Fleur de sel to taste

Sprig of fresh thyme for garnish

Preheat the oven to 375°F.

Lightly brush each slice of bread on both sides with half of the oil. Toast the bread in the preheated oven until the edges begin to turn brown, 2 to 3 minutes.

Heat the honey, thyme, and lemon zest in a small saucepan over low heat. Spread 2 tablespoons goat cheese on each slice of toast while still warm. Top each piece with 2 prosciutto slices and drizzle the honey mixture over the top. Season with salt and fresh thyme, and serve.

ROASTED FETA WITH HERB HONEY

Serves 4 as a starter

This simple appetizer is packed with flavor. Served with crisp apple slices, a crusty loaf of bread, and a glass of chilled rosé, it is a delicious beginning to a warm-weather lunch. Or, for an unexpected treat, serve it alongside a sampling of other cheeses and some dried fruit in lieu of a traditional dessert.

INGREDIENTS

One 8-ounce block Greek feta, blotted dry
2 tablespoons extra-virgin olive oil
2 tablespoons thyme honey or rosemary honey
1 teaspoon freshly ground black pepper
Fresh thyme sprig for garnish

Preheat the oven to 400°F.

Place the feta in a small ovenproof pan lined with aluminum foil or parchment paper. Brush the feta with the olive oil. Bake the cheese until it is soft to the touch but not melted, 8 to 10 minutes. Remove from the oven and set aside.

Preheat the broiler.

Drizzle the baked feta with the honey, then use a pastry brush to spread it over the surface of the cheese. Place the pan under the broiler and bake until the top of the cheese turns brown and starts to bubble. Watch closely so that it does not burn. Season with pepper, add a sprig of thyme, and serve immediately.

HONEY, TAHINI, AND SESAME SEED COOKIES

Makes 24 cookies

These delightful cookies are reminiscent of old-fashioned peanut butter cookies. Like peanut butter, tahini lends a creamy, nutty flavor, and the honey adds a touch of sweetness. If you can find avocado honey, it will add complex warm notes to the cookies. This recipe was inspired by the tahini cookies from Mamaleh's Delicatessen in Cambridge, Massachusetts.

INGREDIENTS

2 cups unbleached all-purpose flour

1 teaspoon baking powder

½ teaspoon kosher salt

1½ sticks (12 tablespoons) unsalted butter, at room temperature

¾ cup sugar

3 tablespoons plus 1½ teaspoons honey, preferably avocado honey

¾ cup tahini

⅓ cup toasted sesame seeds

Preheat the oven to 350°F. Line two baking sheets with parchment paper and set aside.

Whisk together the flour, baking powder, and salt in a medium bowl and set aside.

In a large bowl beat together the butter, sugar, and honey with an electric mixer on medium speed. Continue until the batter is light and fluffy, about 3 minutes. Beat in the tahini, then add the flour mixture in small amounts, beating to combine between additions, until the dough is fully combined. The dough will be slightly sticky.

Place the toasted sesame seeds on a small plate or in a flat bowl. Scoop a heaping tablespoon of dough and roll it into a ball. Dip the top of the ball in the sesame seeds, pressing down to adhere them to the dough. Place the ball of dough seed-side up on one of the prepared baking sheets. Repeat with the remaining dough and seeds, leaving about 2 inches between cookies.

Bake the cookies until golden brown, 13 to 15 minutes. They will expand slightly and flatten as they bake. Allow the cookies to cool on the baking sheets. As they cool, the cookies will become firm.

ISOT PEPPER

ISOT PEPPER IS ONE OF MY FAVORITE SPICES. This chile flake is prized for its dark burgundy color and an intense flavor that adds chocolate undertones and gentle heat to almost any recipe. Not only is it eye-catching when sprinkled on food, but it can be used as a substitute for red pepper flakes, smoked paprika, and hot paprika.

Also known as Urfa biber, isot pepper is grown in the Urfa region of southern Turkey near the Syrian border. It begins as a red, elongated sweet pepper with a mild heat that is partially dried under the summer sun, then covered with fabric and left to ferment and oxidize through the autumn. The dried chiles are crushed into asymmetrical flakes and preserved with oil and salt. During the drying process, the heat of the peppers deepens, producing a flavorful spice that is smoky, spicy, and sour.

BUYING AND STORING ISOT PEPPER

Isot pepper can be found in specialty grocery stores and online. Properly stored, in an airtight container in the pantry away from light and heat, isot pepper retains its potency for eight to ten months.

COOKING WITH ISOT PEPPER

The mild flavor of isot pepper is reminiscent of the ancho chile, but with an earthier taste with hints of espresso and chocolate. Prized for creating a slow-building heat, it deepens the flavors of almost any dish. Because the flakes are packed with salt, you can decrease the amount of salt called for in recipes where it is used.

While in Turkey isot pepper is traditionally used in kebabs and stews, the possible flavor combinations are endless. For an unconventional twist, try adding isot pepper to braised meats, raw oysters, poached eggs, roasted vegetables, salad dressings, popcorn, or a savory fruit compote. It also pairs particularly well with cumin, sumac, paprika, and za'atar. Adding isot pepper to rich desserts softens their sweetness and gives them a pleasing edge.

ISOT PEPPER–SPICED CHICKPEA, FETA, AND POACHED EGG HASH

Serves 4

This one-skillet recipe is my take on shakshuka, a dish that typically consists of poached eggs on a bed of tomatoes, peppers, onions, and garlic. I like to use chickpeas in place of tomatoes. Packed with protein and flavor, this hearty dish pairs perfectly with crusty bread. Serve it for breakfast, brunch, lunch, or dinner.

INGREDIENTS

Three 15.5-ounce cans chickpeas

3 tablespoons avocado oil

4 small shallots, finely diced

1 tablespoon isot pepper

2 teaspoons ground cumin

½ teaspoon kosher salt

½ teaspoon freshly ground black pepper

Zest of ½ lemon

¼ cup freshly squeezed lemon juice

8 large eggs

½ cup crumbled feta

Chopped flat-leaf parsley leaves for garnish

Fresh thyme sprigs for garnish

Drain the chickpeas in a strainer, then rinse, drain, and pat dry thoroughly with paper towels. Set aside.

Heat the oil in a 12-inch cast-iron skillet over medium-high heat. Once the oil is hot, add the chickpeas and stir to coat. Continue cooking, stirring constantly, until the chickpeas are golden brown, 6 to 8 minutes.

Reduce the heat to medium. Add the shallots, isot pepper, cumin, salt, black pepper, and lemon zest and juice. Stir and allow the ingredients to heat through.

Using a spoon, create eight divots in the chickpea mixture. Crack 1 egg into each divot. Cover and cook over medium-low heat until the whites are just set but the yolks are still runny, 8 to 10 minutes. Uncover, remove from the heat, and sprinkle with feta. Garnish with parsley and thyme sprigs, and serve immediately.

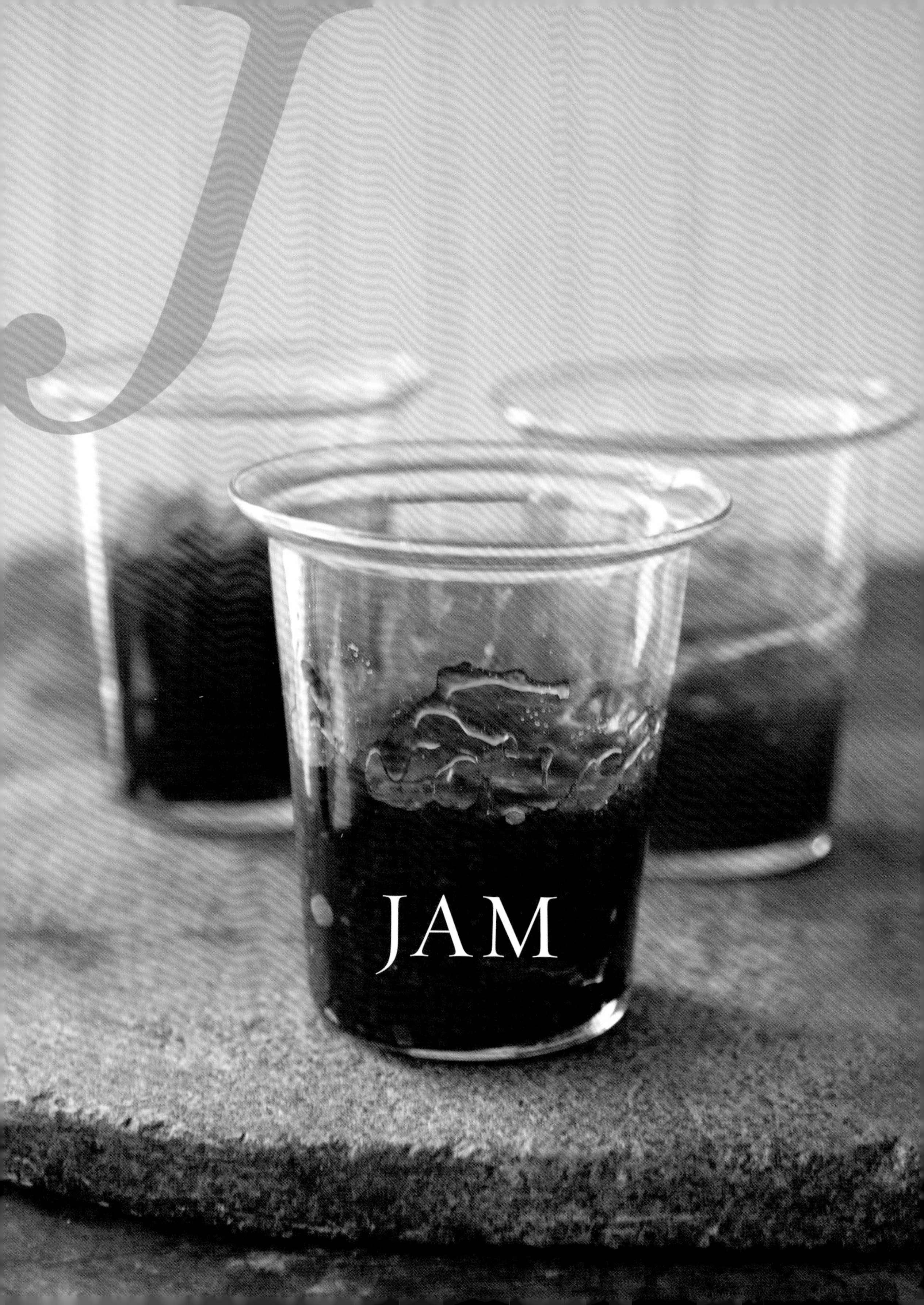

JAM

WHILE I AM NOT A HUGE FAN OF JELLY, jam is an entirely different story. This thick mixture of crushed fruit and sugar, traditionally served with sweet scones or warm slices of buttery toast, is endlessly versatile. It pairs beautifully with cheese, adds a punch of flavor to cookies, perks up poultry, and even enlivens cocktails.

Beyond the standard fruit varieties, some unexpected flavor assortments and savory selections are available and worth trying. For beautiful and unusual jams, you can never go wrong with Stone Hollow Farmstead. The tomato-vanilla jam may sound like an unlikely duo but mixed into a rich Bolognese sauce its earthy sweetness serves as a fantastic foil to acidic tomatoes. For zesty flavors, I often reach for Robert Rothschild. From smoky fig and roasted garlic to balsamic caramelized onion to hot pepper peach, these delicious products add an unexpected twist to many dishes. After browning a tenderloin, I often add a splash of red wine and a Robert Rothschild savory jam to the skillet to deglaze the pan or create a rich reduction.

CREATIVE WAYS TO USE JAM

Rather then letting a jar of jam languish in the refrigerator, try these ideas for a new twist on your repertoire of recipes. The possibilities are limitless.

A grilled Gruyère cheese sandwich with raspberry jam is a nod to the traditional pairing of sweet spreads and sharp cheeses.

Fragrant, tangy, and bursting with umami goodness, tomato jam transforms English muffins. Top each muffin with a dollop of jam, fresh spinach, a hot poached egg, and fresh herbs.

Peach jam blended with Worcestershire sauce, garlic powder, Tabasco sauce, vinegar, and brown sugar creates the groundwork for a killer barbecue sauce.

For a refreshing gin cocktail, mix 1 tablespoon blackberry jam, the juice of half a lemon, and two shots of gin or vodka in a cocktail shaker (or a small jar with a fitted lid). Shake to combine the ingredients. Strain, pour over ice, and serve with fresh blackberries.

AROMATIC APRICOT CHICKEN WITH CASHEWS

Serves 4 to 6

This lightly spiced and fragrant dish, filled with tender chicken, jam, and sticky apricots is simple to prepare. For an elegant meal, serve it with a green salad and basmati rice or couscous.

INGREDIENTS

1 tablespoon grapeseed or light olive oil

2 large yellow onions, thinly sliced

1½ teaspoons ground cinnamon

1 teaspoon ground turmeric

1 teaspoon ground ginger

1 teaspoon ground cumin

¼ teaspoon ground allspice

4 boneless, skinless chicken breasts, cubed

2 cups chicken stock

12 dried apricots

2 tablespoons apricot jam

⅓ cup lightly salted cashews, chopped

Chopped fresh cilantro leaves for garnish

Heat the oil in a large saucepan over medium and cook the onions, stirring frequently, until soft and translucent, 3 to 4 minutes. Add the spices and the chicken and stir to coat evenly and distribute the spices. Add the stock and bring to a boil.

Reduce the heat to medium-low, cover, and simmer for 15 minutes, stirring occasionally. Add the apricots and simmer for another 15 minutes. Remove the lid, stir in the jam, and continue cooking for 10 additional minutes.

Transfer to a serving dish. Top with the cashews and garnish with cilantro. Serve hot.

KECAP MANIS

KECAP MANIS, PRONOUNCED KEH-CHUP MAH-NEESE (and also spelled ketjap manis) is a thick, sweet soy sauce traditionally used in Indonesian fare. The most popular condiment in Indonesia, it also stars in the cuisines of Malaysia and Singapore. Made from sugar and soybeans, it has a unique zest that imparts a savory caramel soy sauce taste.

This umami flavor is used in the most popular Indonesian dishes, including nasi goreng (fried rice), mie goreng (spicy fried noodles), kwetiau goreng (fried flat noodles), semur (beef stew), and ketoprak (vermicelli and tofu).

Kecap manis can be purchased online and in most Asian supermarkets. However, if you are like me and the door of your refrigerator is on the verge of collapse from the collection of condiments, you can make your own in small amounts.

HOMEMADE KECAP MANIS
Makes ½ cup sauce

½ cup soy sauce
½ cup brown sugar

In a small saucepan, combine the soy sauce and brown sugar. Bring to a boil over medium heat. Continue to cook at a gentle simmer until the mixture thickens and resembles maple syrup. Keep an eye on it while it cooks to avoid it boiling over. Remove from the heat to cool. As the mixture cools down, it will further thicken.

Kept in a sealed container, kecap manis will last in the refrigerator for up to one year. Bring it to room temperature before using in a recipe or as a dipping sauce.

For variation, I often use Bragg liquid aminos in place of the soy sauce for less sodium, and I sometimes use ponzu sauce. This classic Japanese condiment offers a tangy citrus flavor.

HOW TO USE KECAP MANIS
I love kecap manis swirled into Vietnamese pho, as a dipping sauce for dumplings, and mixed into a cold soba noodle salad. However, you need not restrict your use of kecap manis to Asian dishes, as it can brighten almost any recipe. I have found it delicious in marinated beef, slow-cooked pork with ginger, sticky glazed ribs, and braised duck.

CHICKEN SATAY WITH KECAP MANIS AND PEANUT SAUCE

Serves 4 to 6 as an entrée

Juicy pieces of chicken marinated in homemade kecap manis, threaded onto wooden skewers, and grilled to perfection are simply delicious. Serve this Indonesian classic with creamy spiced peanut sauce for an easy and charming meal.

INGREDIENTS

¼ cup plus 2 tablespoons kecap manis

¼ cup plus 2 tablespoons freshly squeezed lime juice

1½ tablespoons coconut oil

1½ pounds boneless skinless chicken breasts, cut into 1-inch pieces

½ cup creamy peanut butter

1 tablespoon Thai fish sauce

1 small fresh Thai chile pepper, finely chopped

2 cloves garlic, minced

¼ cup lightly salted peanuts, roughly chopped

Peanut oil for grilling

Fresh minced parsely for garnish

Soak 8 to 10 bamboo skewers in water for at least 30 minutes.

In a large bowl, combine ¼ cup of the kecap manis, 3 tablespoons of the lime juice, and the coconut oil. Add the chicken pieces to the bowl and toss to coat. Cover with plastic wrap and refrigerate for 10 minutes.

In a small bowl, whisk together the peanut butter, the remaining 2 tablespoons kecap manis, the remaining 3 tablespoons lime juice, the fish sauce, the chile pepper, and the garlic. While whisking constantly, add 2 tablespoons water in a thin stream. Whisk until the mixture is emulsified. Stir in the peanuts.

Thread 3 to 4 pieces of the marinated chicken on each skewer. Brush the skewered chicken with the marinade remaining in the bowl.

Preheat a grill to medium heat. If needed, lightly oil the grate. Place the skewers on the grill. Cook for 8 minutes, flip, and continue cooking until the chicken is lightly charred and cooked through, or until the chicken reaches an internal temperature of 165°F, about 8 additional minutes.

Garnish with fresh parsley and serve immediately with the peanut sauce.

LENTILS

EASY TO COOK, VERSATILE, AND INEXPENSIVE, lentils are one of the most humble and useful dry goods in the pantry. Unlike dried beans, lentils do not need to be soaked before cooking. While small in size, they are packed with protein and fiber.

Simplicity aside, they are one of my favorite staples. From stews and soups to salads and even desserts, these pulses are a kitchen mainstay. Fantastic on their own, they also shine alongside braised meats and are a perfect companion to roasted vegetables. When I am in need of an interesting vegetarian dish, or just looking for something that is fast, hearty, and healthy, lentils never fail.

LENTIL VARIETIES

While lentils come in several varieties, the five main types are brown, green, red, black, and French.

Brown lentils are the most common type found on supermarket shelves. Ready to eat in 20 minutes, they possess a mild, earthy flavor and range in color from taupe to dark brown. Brown lentils are best used in veggie burgers, casseroles, and stews.

Green lentils offer a robust and slightly peppery flavor. Similar to brown lentils in size, they take longer to cook and hold their shape, making them a great choice for salads and pilafs.

Red lentils are split and hulled legumes. Much like other hulled pulses, such as yellow peas, green peas, pigeon peas, and mung beans, they quickly melt when they are cooked. Their creamy consistency is perfect for soup.

Black lentils are eye-catching on a plate or in a bowl. Resembling caviar, they are also referred to as beluga lentils. These black beauties are rich in flavor, hold their shape, and have the highest protein count of all the varieties. A wonderful choice for dramatic side dishes, pilafs, or casseroles, they are a personal favorite.

French lentils are a variety of green lentils. What sets them apart from standard green lentils is their darker color and smaller size, and especially their mineral and earthy flavor. The most popular French lentil is the Puy lentil, hailing from Le Puy in central France. This famed town is surrounded by a volcanic plateau, which contributes to the lentils' flavor. Grown in the region since the seventeenth century, Puy lentils carry the prestigious AOC (Appellation d'Origine Contrôllée) seal. The French government stamp not only indicates the quality of the product, but also guarantees the conditions of the growing area.

MOROCCAN-INSPIRED LENTIL AND RAISIN SOUP

Serves 4 as a main course or starter

Moroccan cuisine is known for its heady mixture of spices, sweet aromatic scents, and dried fruits. This soup is my vegetarian take on a traditional tagine. The recipe was inspired by a lovely soup featured on the beautiful blog *Feasting at Home*.

INGREDIENTS

2 tablespoons extra-virgin olive oil

1 medium yellow onion, diced

3 carrots, diced

1 small sweet potato, peeled and diced

1 teaspoon kosher salt, plus more to taste

6 cloves garlic, minced

½ cup jarred roasted red peppers, drained and diced

2 teaspoons ground cumin

½ teaspoon freshly ground black pepper, plus more to taste

½ teaspoon chili powder

½ teaspoon ground cinnamon

½ teaspoon ground turmeric

¼ teaspoon red pepper flakes

One 14-ounce can fire-roasted diced tomatoes

4 cups vegetable broth

2 bay leaves (fresh, if available)

1 teaspoon honey

¾ cup red lentils, rinsed and drained

¼ cup quinoa

¼ cup black raisins

¼ cup golden raisins

¼ cup roasted sunflower seeds

Leaves of 1 sprig cilantro, minced

Heat the oil in a large stockpot over medium-low. Add the onion, carrots, sweet potato, and the 1 teaspoon salt. Cover and cook for 10 minutes, stirring occasionally, until the vegetables have softened; but do not allow them to brown.

Add the garlic and the roasted red peppers. Cook for an additional 3 minutes. Stir in the cumin, ½ teaspoon black pepper, chili powder, cinnamon, turmeric, and red pepper flakes. Add the diced tomatoes, broth, and bay leaves. Stir and bring to a low boil. Add the honey, lentils, quinoa, and raisins.

Lower the heat to a gentle simmer and cover. Cook until the lentils are tender, about 12 minutes. Taste and adjust the salt and black pepper, if needed. Remove and discard the bay leaves. Divide the soup among four soup plates. Garnish each serving with 1 tablespoon sunflower seeds and a bit of the cilantro.

WARM LENTIL SALAD WITH CELERY AND MEDJOOL DATES

Serves 6 as a side dish or a light main course

Sweet dates, tangy lemon, warming cumin, crunchy Marcona almonds, salty pecorino Romano, and Puy lentils transform this humble celery salad by offering an explosion of flavor.

INGREDIENTS

¾ cup Puy lentils

¼ teaspoon kosher salt, plus more to taste

¼ cup freshly squeezed lemon juice

¼ cup extra-virgin olive oil

2 teaspoons honey

I teaspoon ground cumin

⅛ teaspoon red pepper flakes

8 ribs celery, thinly sliced on a diagonal

6 medjool dates, pitted and roughly chopped

3 scallions, white and pale green parts sliced on a diagonal

½ cup Marcona almonds, roughly chopped

¼ cup grated Parmigiano Reggiano

¼ cup grated pecorino Romano

Fresh celery leaves for garnish

Rinse the lentils. Transfer them to a stockpot and add 3 cups of water and salt to taste. Bring the water to a boil, cover the pot, and simmer gently until the lentils are tender, 20 to 25 minutes. Drain the lentils, set aside, and allow them to cool slightly.

In a small bowl, whisk together the lemon juice, olive oil, honey, cumin, ¼ teaspoon salt, and red pepper flakes. Set the vinaigrette aside.

In a large bowl, combine the celery, dates, scallions, almonds, and lentils. Gently toss the salad with the vinaigrette.

Transfer the salad to a large platter and top with the Parmigiano, pecorino, and celery leaves.

LEMON-LENTIL SOUP

Serves 4 to 6 as a main course or starter

This is my go-to soup. Any time I feel unwell or crave comfort food, I whip up a pot of it. Chock-full of lentils and carrot and scented with lemon and turmeric, it is savory, satisfying, and utterly delicious. For this recipe I sweat my vegetables, cooking them until they are softened without browning them. A technique called à l'étouffée in French cooking, it adds depth of flavor to the soup.

INGREDIENTS

1 tablespoon extra-light olive oil
2 cups finely chopped yellow onion
2 cups chopped carrot
1¼ teaspoons kosher salt
3 cloves garlic, minced
2 teaspoons ground cumin
1 teaspoon ground turmeric
½ teaspoon ground coriander

½ teaspoon freshly ground black pepper
½ teaspoon mild curry powder
⅛ teaspoon cayenne
2 cups red lentils, rinsed and drained
8 cups chicken or vegetable broth
Juice of 1 large lemon
Flat-leaf parsley for granish

Heat the oil in a large stockpot over medium-low. Add the onions, carrots, and ¼ teaspoon of the salt. Cook the vegetables without browning, stirring frequently, until they are soft and sweet smelling, 8 to 10 minutes. Stir in the garlic, cumin, turmeric, coriander, black pepper, curry powder, cayenne, and remaining 1 teaspoon salt and cook for 30 seconds.

Stir in the lentils and broth. Increase the heat to high and bring to a boil. Reduce the heat to a simmer and cook, partially covered, until the lentils are tender, 20 to 25 minutes. Remove the soup from the heat. Stir in the lemon juice, garnish with parsley, and serve.

FINE
DE
DiJON

Poupon

MUSTARD

I LOVE MUSTARD. Though many enjoy it served with hot dogs or as a dip for soft pretzels, I like to mix it into vinaigrettes or use it as the foundation for mosterdsoep, a creamy Dutch mustard soup filled with leeks and topped with pancetta. A hint of this versatile aromatic condiment elevates many other dishes as well. Not only does mustard help to create a beautiful crust for a leg of lamb or flavor a potato salad and deviled eggs, it can also be used to cut through the creaminess of mashed potatoes and to brighten soups and stews. For breakfast I love mixing Dijon mustard with a splash of half-and-half and a squirt of lemon and pouring it over sunny-side-up eggs, and in the summer I make a mustard-coated pastry crust for a tomato and Camembert tart.

When a dish tastes as if something is missing, many will reach for the salt. However, I learned from chef Vivian Howard that acid is most likely the missing element. Adding mustard—or another acid, like lemon juice or vinegar—helps balance the flavor of food, teases out the aromas, and brings all of the flavors into sharper focus.

TYPES OF MUSTARD

Several outstanding mustards are available at markets. I am a huge fan of the Maille brand, especially their horseradish mustard. When shopping for mustard, select one that is minimally processed with only a handful of ingredients, so that the true flavor shines through.

Yellow: One of the mildest mustards, yellow mustard is hugely popular in the United States, particularly at backyard barbecues. Its characteristically bright yellow color comes from turmeric.

Dijon: This classic French mustard is often made with white wine and brown or black mustard seeds. It is more pungent and spicier than yellow mustard. Hailing from the Dijon region of France, it has a sharp taste that works particularly well in vinaigrettes.

Spicy brown: Slightly coarser than yellow or Dijon, this type of mustard mainly consists of brown mustard seeds, which deliver more heat than yellow or white seeds. Its deep flavor stands up well to rich, salty meats like pastrami, corned beef, and sausages.

Whole-grain: Sometimes called grainy stone ground or coarse ground, this mustard is prepared with both whole and ground seeds. It is delightful paired with roasted vegetables and new potatoes.

HOMEMADE MUSTARD
Makes 1 cup

Homemade mustard is delicious and easy to make.

¼ cup brown mustard seeds
¼ cup yellow mustard seeds
⅔ cup dry white wine
½ cup white wine vinegar
1 teaspoon kosher salt

Place the mustard seeds in a medium bowl. Stir in the wine and vinegar. Cover with plastic wrap and allow the mixture to sit at room temperature for 24 hours.

In a blender, blend the mixture with the salt until smooth. Add a few drops of water if the consistency is too thick.

Transfer to an airtight container and refrigerate for at least 48 hours before using.

BISTRO SALAD WITH ROASTED VEGETABLES AND MUSTARD VINAIGRETTE

Serves 4

Inspired by classic French bistro salads, this hearty salad is perfect for an autumn or winter lunch.

INGREDIENTS

3 large carrots, peeled and cut into 1-inch pieces

2 large parsnips, peeled and cut into 1-inch pieces

1 rutabaga, peeled and cut into 1-inch pieces

½ cup extra-virgin olive oil

1 teaspoon kosher salt

2 teaspoons freshly ground black pepper

1 clove garlic, grated

1 teaspoon smoked paprika

3 tablespoons whole-grain mustard

2 tablespoons sherry vinegar

6 cups mesclun greens, or an herb salad mix

½ cup toasted walnuts, coarsely chopped

¼ cup crumbled goat cheese

Fleur de sel to taste

Preheat the oven to 425°F.

In a large bowl, toss the vegetables with ¼ cup of the olive oil and season with the kosher salt and 1½ teaspoons pepper. Spread the vegetables on a large baking sheet and roast. Stir the vegetables every 10 to 15 minutes. Continue roasting until the vegetables are easily pierced with a fork and brown around the edges.

In a medium bowl, whisk together the garlic, paprika, mustard, vinegar, and the remaining ¼ cup olive oil and ½ teaspoon pepper to create the dressing.

Place the roasted vegetables and greens in a large bowl. Add the dressing and toss to combine. Transfer to a large platter and top with walnuts, goat cheese, and a pinch of fleur de sel. Serve immediately.

NUTMEG

NUTMEG HAS A LONG HISTORY of providing a warm and nutty aroma to foods. Much like cinnamon and allspice, it is intense and fragrant. Just a pinch adds bold flavor to everything from sweet desserts to seasonal beverages, tasty winter gratins, and squash soups. For me, it is the quintessential spice for fall and winter. Béchamel, spinach gnocchi, creamed spinach, pumpkin waffles, maple-roasted Brussels sprouts, scalloped potatoes, rich soufflés—each benefits from its subtle heat.

Contrary to its name and nutty flavor, nutmeg is not a tree nut but rather a seed from a tropical evergreen tree that is native to Indonesia. Specifically, it is the seed inside of the bright red seed covering from which mace is made.

GROUND VERSUS WHOLE

There is no question that pre-ground nutmeg is a convenient choice; however, nothing beats the flavor of freshly ground whole nutmeg. Though it is quite fragrant when you first open the jar, ground nutmeg loses its potency very quickly.

Whole nutmeg seeds are about the size of plum pits and are usually sold six to eight in a jar. To use, grate with a microplane zester or spice grinder. Unlike ground nutmeg, whole seeds will last indefinitely if they are stored away from heat and moisture.

NUTMEG IN DISHES AROUND THE WORLD

Some people dismiss nutmeg as cinnamon's country cousin, used only in eggnog, cakes, or cookies. Nothing could be further from the truth. This pleasantly pungent seed is found in a myriad of dishes around the world. Native to Indonesia, nutmeg is frequently added to soups, stews, and curries in that country. The key flavor in oxtail soup, it is also prevalent in rendang curry, where it cuts the richness of the coconut milk. In Italy, nutmeg is the star of beloved mortadella, and a pinch is often sprinkled into the filling for soft ravioli. In Indian cuisine, nutmeg is added to savory spice blends, such as garam masala, and in Scotland it is traditionally used to make savory meat puddings.

FOOD PAIRINGS

Nutmeg pairs nicely with a wide variety of foods, herbs, and spices. The next time you are in the kitchen try one of these suggestions:

Sprinkle it over avocados instead of red pepper flakes and add a squeeze of lemon juice.

Stir a little into cooked vegetables, such as sweet or russet potatoes, carrots, pumpkin, winter squash, cauliflower, and spinach.

There is no question that most fruits are delicious on their own. To further enhance their flavor, try a dusting of nutmeg over apples, peaches, pears, or mango.

It is impossible not to think of nutmeg and eggnog mingled in a mug served at Christmastime. But do not wait until the holidays to enjoy the spice. Add a little nutmeg to a cup of coffee, hot chocolate, tea, or cider.

CREAMY NUTMEG-SPIKED GRATIN

Serves 6

Admittedly, this gratin is not a dish that my waistline can regularly tolerate. But a few times a year—on a cold rainy day or for a Christmas Eve supper—it is a delicious treat. The thinly sliced potatoes spiked with nutmeg and cream soak up lots of flavor.

INGREDIENTS

3 tablespoons unsalted butter

3 leeks, thinly sliced

1 medium yellow onion, thinly sliced

1½ teaspoons kosher salt

½ teaspoon white pepper

3 cloves garlic, thinly sliced

Leaves of 2 fresh thyme sprigs, minced

2 cups canned artichoke hearts, drained and quartered

3 large russet potatoes, very thinly sliced

2 pounds cod loin, cut into bite-size pieces

1½ cups grated Gruyère or Emmental

1½ cups heavy cream

½ teaspoon freshly grated nutmeg

½ teaspoon ground cayenne pepper

½ cup grated Parmigiano Reggiano

Fresh thyme sprigs for garnish

Preheat the oven to 425°F.

Butter a 3-quart baking dish with 1 tablespoon of the butter and set aside. Melt the remaining 2 tablespoons butter in a large skillet over medium heat. Add the leeks, onion, 1 teaspoon of the salt, and the pepper. Stir and cover. Continue cooking, stirring occasionally until tender, 6 to 8 minutes. Add the garlic, thyme, and artichokes and cook an additional 2 minutes. Then remove from the heat.

In the prepared baking dish, layer one-third of the potato slices. Top with half of the artichoke mixture, all of the cod, and half of the Gruyère. Layer with another one-third of the potatoes and top with half of the artichoke mixture. Top with the remaining potatoes and cheese.

Pour the heavy cream into a small bowl and add the nutmeg, cayenne pepper, and the remaining ½ teaspoon salt. Mix well. Pour the heavy cream mixture over the potatoes. Sprinkle on the Parmigiano.

Tightly cover the baking dish with aluminum foil. Bake for 40 minutes. Remove the foil and bake until the potatoes are tender, and the top is golden brown, another 30 to 35 minutes. Let the gratin rest 5 to 10 minutes. Garnish with fresh thyme and serve.

OATS

WHAT COULD BE BETTER than a warm bowl of oatmeal on a cool crisp morning? Yet, while oatmeal serves as a healthy and hearty morning meal, oats are not just for breakfast. This versatile grain with many benefits can be incorporated into everything from fritters to savory sundried tomato muffins.

Like all grains, oats are made up of kernels with three parts: the bran layer, filled with fiber and vitamins; the germ, rich in healthy oils; and the starchy endosperm, containing more protein per serving than most whole-grain cereals. Oats are also rich in potassium, low in sodium, and contain several vitamins, including thiamin, riboflavin, niacin, vitamins B6 and E, and folate.

TYPES OF OATS

All oats start off as groats, the whole unbroken kernels of the oat. Before being processed into different varieties, the groats are roasted at a very low temperature.

QUICK-ROLLED OATS, also referred to as instant oats, go through the most processing—they are partially cooked with steam, then flattened until very thin—and as a result cook quite quickly. They have a mild flavor and retain less texture than other forms of oats. Similar to rolled oats, they are steamed longer and rolled thinner.

ROLLED OATS, also called old-fashioned oats, are oat groats that have been run through a roller, giving them their signature flat shape. Before being flattened, they are steamed to create softness and pliability. Rolled oats cook much faster than unrolled oats and absorb more liquid. They are commonly used in muesli, cookies, muffins, and other baked goods.

SCOTTISH OATS are whole groats that have been ground (preferably stone-ground) into a meal rather than being cut with a blade. Their texture is similar to that of steel-cut oats, but finer, and their consistency makes for a creamy and nutty porridge.

STEEL-CUT OATS, also known as Irish oats, are groats that have been cut into small pieces with a sharp metal blade. They take the longest time to cook and have a chewy texture because the pieces retain their shape after cooking. In addition to porridge, steel-cut oats can be used to bind meatloaf or add texture to stuffing.

FUN FACT

Each fall, oatmeal fans from around the world gather in the small village of Carrbridge, Scotland. They trek to the Highlands with a lofty, yet humble objective—to be named the World Porridge Making Champion and take home the Golden Spurtle trophy. The rules are strict. Each bowl of porridge is made with nothing more than oats, water, and salt. Competitors often bring their own water and select their salt with equal care.

No electricity is supplied, and contestants rely on their own cooking devices. The implements are spartan, too, consisting of just a pot and a spurtle. This wooden Scottish kitchen tool, dating from the fifteenth century, is used to stir porridge. The rodlike shape allows porridge to be stirred without forming lumps. Spoons are deemed to have a dragging effect.

PESTO AND ROASTED POTATO OATMEAL BOWLS

Serves 4 as a main course

I love this nourishing and savory bowl of oatmeal, studded with roasted garlic and topped with crispy potatoes and bright basil pesto. Serve it for breakfast, lunch, or dinner. If you like, top each portion with an egg cooked sunny-side up.

INGREDIENTS

1½ pounds small new potatoes, cut into ½-inch wedges

1 tablespoon plus 1½ teaspoons sea salt

8 cloves garlic, unpeeled

2 tablespoons extra-virgin olive oil

2 cups rolled oats

1 cup shredded Gruyère

¼ cup basil pesto, preferably Seggiano

Fleur de sel to taste

Freshly ground black pepper to taste

Preheat the oven to 425°F. Line a baking sheet with parchment paper and set aside.

Place the potatoes in a large stockpot and add enough cold water to cover by 1 inch. Add 1 tablespoon of the sea salt and bring the water to a boil over medium heat. Boil for 4 minutes, then drain the potatoes.In a medium bowl, toss the potato wedges and garlic cloves in the oil with the remaining 1½ teaspoons sea salt.

Spread the potatoes and garlic in a single layer on the prepared baking sheet. Roast in the preheated oven for 10 minutes, then remove the garlic cloves. Once the garlic is cool enough to handle, peel the cloves (just squeeze them and they should pop out of the skin) and set aside. Meanwhile, toss the potatoes and roast them until golden brown, about 10 additional minutes.

While the potatoes are in the oven, bring 4 cups water to a boil in a large saucepan over high heat. Once the water is boiling, stir in the oats and lower the heat to medium-high. Cook for 5 minutes, stirring occasionally. Once the oats are cooked, fold in the cheese. Stir until the cheese is melted and the oats are creamy. Divide the oatmeal among four bowls. Top each portion with potatoes, 1 tablespoon pesto, and 2 cloves roasted garlic. Season with fleur de sel and pepper to taste.

OATMEAL SODA BREAD

Makes 1 loaf

This bread is perfect slathered with Irish butter or dunked into a steamy bowl of stew. Made from humble ingredients, it can be ready to eat in an hour, and it is best eaten immediately after baking.

INGREDIENTS

2 cups rolled oats

2¼ cups unbleached all-purpose flour, plus more for dusting

2 teaspoons baking soda

2 teaspoons sugar

1 teaspoon kosher salt

1½ cups buttermilk

1 large egg, at room temperature

Butter for greasing the skillet

Preheat the oven to 450°F.

Place the oats in a food processor fitted with the metal blade. Pulse until they are finely ground.

In a large bowl, mix the ground oats, 2¼ cups flour, baking soda, sugar, and salt until incorporated. Make a well in the center of the flour mixture with a large spoon.

In a medium bowl, whisk the buttermilk and egg together, then pour the buttermilk mixture into the well.

With the wooden spoon, gently fold the surrounding flour over the buttermilk. Continue to fold until the dough is just combined. Do not overmix. The dough will be on the moist side. If it is too wet to handle, add a little more flour.

Place the dough on a lightly floured surface. Knead only two times to shape it into a mound.

Grease a large cast-iron skillet with butter and put the dough in the center.

Place the skillet in the preheated oven and bake for 15 minutes. Then lower the temperature to 400°F and bake for an additional 25 minutes.

Remove the pan from the oven and allow the bread to cool in the pan for 10 minutes. Then transfer the bread to a wire cooling rack. Let cool for another 10 minutes.

OATCAKES

Makes six 3-inch cakes

One of the things I miss about living in Scotland is picking up oatcakes from the grocery store each week. Luckily, they are easy to make at home. Steel-cut oatmeal and whole wheat flour create savory crackers that are crisp and nutty. I like to eat them with cheese, smoked fish pâté, or cream cheese. They are great with butter and jam, too.

INGREDIENTS

⅔ cup steel-cut oats
¼ cup whole wheat flour
½ teaspoon kosher salt
¼ teaspoon baking soda
1 tablespoon unsalted butter, cold
Unbleached all-purpose flour for work surface

Preheat the oven to 350°F. Line a baking sheet with parchment paper and set aside.

In a large bowl, mix together the oats, flour, salt, and baking soda. Cut in the butter until it is evenly distributed. Add 3 tablespoons cold water and mix with a fork just until moist.

On a lightly floured surface, pat the dough into a ball and flatten it slightly. Roll out the dough to a ¼-inch thickness. Cut into rounds with a 3-inch cookie cutter. Reroll the scraps and cut more rounds.

Place the rounds ¼ inch apart on the prepared baking sheet. Bake in the preheated oven until they are slightly firm and lightly golden, 15 to 20 minutes. Transfer the oatcakes to a rack and allow them to cool before serving.

NORDIC ROOT VEGETABLE SOUP

Serves 4 to 6 as a main course

Oats are not just for baking or breakfast. They are a great addition to brothy soups. This recipe is my take on the root vegetable soups that I have enjoyed in Denmark and Iceland. Both countries have a long culinary history of using winter roots to create robust meals. The oats are a nod to my mother's barley vegetable soup—nothing fancy, just simple and delicious.

INGREDIENTS

1 cup rolled oats
2 tablespoons extra-virgin olive oil
3 large shallots, thinly sliced
2 leeks, white and tender green parts thinly sliced
4 cloves garlic, minced
8 cups chicken or vegetable stock, plus more if needed
8 sprigs thyme

3 bay leaves
1 pound turnips or rutabagas, cut into ½-inch pieces
½ pound parsnips, peeled and cut into ½-inch pieces
½ pound carrots, peeled and cut into ½-inch pieces
1½ teaspoons kosher salt, plus more to taste
½ teaspoon freshly ground black pepper, plus more to taste
½ teaspoon freshly grated nutmeg
Flat-leaf parsley for garnish

Heat a large skillet over medium-high. Add the oats. Stirring often, toast them until they are fragrant, about 5 minutes. Remove the oats from the heat and set aside.

Heat the oil in a large stockpot over medium-high. Add the shallots and leeks. Sauté until tender, about 5 minutes. Add the garlic and sauté 1 additional minute.

Add the broth, 2 cups water, thyme, and bay leaves, and bring to a boil. Add the turnips, parsnips, carrots, 1½ teaspoons salt, and ½ teaspoon pepper. Simmer over medium-low heat until the vegetables are tender, about 40 minutes. Increase the heat to medium-high and bring to a gentle boil, then add the toasted oats. Stir to combine, lower the heat to medium, and cover. Simmer until the soup is thick, 8 to 10 minutes.

Stir in the nutmeg and allow the soup to simmer, uncovered, for 1 minute. If the soup becomes too thick, add a splash of broth or water. Adjust salt and pepper, if needed, and granish with fresh parsley. Serve in large soup bowls.

OLIVES

OLIVES MAY BE SMALL, BUT THEY ARE MIGHTY IN FLAVOR—and that flavor ranges from vegetal to briny. From the beautiful buttery green varieties to the blissful picholine, my pantry is never without an assortment of olives. There are hundreds of varieties and cultivars around the world, and each possesses a unique shape, size, and color—and a distinctive taste. There is something for every palate.

Olives bring a meaty, briny, and aromatic quality to tapenade, salads, stews, sauces, and, of course, martinis. They pair well with grilled fish, braised beef, and roast chicken. Eaten alone or baked into bread, olives offer a wonderful brightness.

One of the easiest ways to enjoy olives is to marinate them in warm olive oil with fresh rosemary, bay leaves, lemon zest, and peppercorns. They are delectable served aside a cheeseboard or presented as a hostess gift. When it comes to olives, you cannot go wrong.

PERFECT PAIRINGS

Different cheese, olive, and wine combinations offer complex tastes. Here are my favorite pairings:

French Picholine olives are brine-cured, citrusy, and crisp. Pair them with brie and sauvignon blanc.

Spanish Manzanilla olives are the classic martini olive. Plump and firm with meaty texture, they are both briny and bitter. Pair them with Manchego and Spanish cava or fino sherry.

Italian Cerignola olives hail from the Puglia region. Large and meaty, they boast a buttery and sweet taste. Pair them with Parmigiano Reggiano and prosecco or pinot grigio.

Sicilian Castelvetrano olives are known for their gorgeous green color. Irresistibly sweet and buttery, they are a personal favorite. Pair them with an aged pecorino or Asiago, accompanied by a glass of pinot grigio or sauvignon blanc.

Greek Kalamata olives are rich with an intensely fruity flavor. They range in color from purple to black. Pair them with feta and pinot noir or a dry Greek wine.

California Sevillano olives are plump and green, offering a crisp, meaty, briny bite. Pair them with goat cheese and cabernet franc or Barolo.

Niçoise olives are synonymous with the cuisine of southern France. Fragrant and firm, these purplish-brown olives have a slightly sour flavor. Pair them with Camembert and Chardonnay.

FIG TAPENADE AND CHÈVRE CROSTINI

Serves 4 to 6 as a starter

Made with dried figs, kalamata olives, and capers, this savory appetizer has been adapted from *The Yellow Table* by Anna Watson Carl. The sweet and salty tapenade is the perfect foil for tangy goat cheese. If you are serving these on a platter, garnish with a few fresh thyme sprigs.

INGREDIENTS

I small baguette, thinly sliced

3 tablespoons extra-virgin olive oil

12 dried black mission or Calimyrna figs, stemmed and halved

½ cup Kalamata olives, pitted

1½ teaspoons capers, rinsed and drained

I tablespoon fresh thyme leaves, plus sprigs for garnish

2 teaspoons balsamic vinegar

¼ teaspoon kosher salt, plus more to taste

Freshly ground black pepper to taste

One 8-ounce log goat cheese

Preheat the oven to 425°F.

Brush the bread slices on both sides with 1 tablespoon of the oil and arrange on a baking sheet. Bake in the preheated oven until golden brown, 3 to 5 minutes. Remove from the oven and allow to cool slightly.

Place the figs, olives, capers, and thyme leaves in the bowl of a food processor fitted with the metal blade and pulse until coarse. Add the vinegar, remaining 2 tablespoons oil, and ¼ teaspoon salt and pulse until combined. Season with pepper and more salt, if needed.

Spread some of the goat cheese on each slice of bread. Top each with a spoonful of tapenade, thyme, and serve.

GREEN APPLE AND CASTELVETRANO SPRING SALAD

Serves 4 to 6 as a side dish

While apples and olives may seem an unlikely combination, the tart salty and herbal notes of this salad are surprisingly refreshing. In the autumn, try it with radicchio and late-season apples, such as pink lady or gala.

INGREDIENTS

¼ cup extra-virgin olive oil

1 tablespoon plus 1½ teaspoons apple cider vinegar

1½ teaspoons honey

1 teaspoon Dijon mustard

½ teaspoon sea salt

Freshly ground black pepper to taste

5 cups spring salad greens

1 large Granny Smith apple, cored and diced

¾ cup Castelvetrano olives, pitted

½ cup Marcona almonds

4 ounces goat cheese, crumbled

Fresh sprigs of oregano for garnish

In a small bowl, whisk together the oil, vinegar, honey, mustard, and salt. Season with pepper. Cover the vinaigrette with plastic wrap and refrigerate for at least 30 minutes to allow the flavors to marry.

Place the greens on a large platter or in a large serving bowl. Just before serving, dice the apples and add them to the salad along with the olives and almonds.

Drizzle the salad with just enough of the vinaigrette to coat lightly. Gently toss. Taste and add more vinaigrette, if needed. Sprinkle with the goat cheese, and fresh oregano, and serve.

NAVY BEAN AND LACINATO KALE STEW WITH FETA AND OLIVES

Serves 6 to 8 as a main course

I could eat this flavorful stew every day. Adapted from an old *Bon Appétit* recipe, it is super easy to make. However, cooking the beans does take forethought. Canned beans will not work for this recipe. Since no stock is used, you need the starch from the beans to achieve a creamy consistency. Serve it with a loaf of crusty bread.

INGREDIENTS

6 cloves garlic, peeled

¼ cup plus 2 tablespoons extra-virgin olive oil

I large yellow onion, diced

2 bulbs fennel, thinly sliced

I teaspoon kosher salt, plus more to taste

3 tablespoons freshly squeezed lemon juice, plus more to taste

3 tablespoons Castelvetrano olive brine

2 tablespoons finely chopped fresh rosemary leaves

½ teaspoon red pepper flakes

3 bay leaves

2 cups dried navy beans, soaked overnight and drained

I cup Castelvetrano olives, pitted

2 bunches lacinato kale, stems removed and roughly chopped

8 ounces feta, crumbled

Smash each garlic clove with the flat side of a large knife and set aside.

Heat the oil in a large stockpot over medium-low heat. Add the garlic and cook, stirring often, until golden but not burnt, about 5 minutes. Add the onion, fennel, and 1 tablespoon salt. Cook, stirring often, until the onion is translucent and the fennel is golden brown, 6 to 10 minutes. Add the 3 tablespoons lemon juice, olive brine, rosemary, and red pepper flakes. Cook, stirring frequently, until the rosemary is fragrant, about 1 minute.

Add the bay leaves, beans, and 8 cups water and bring to a simmer. Partially cover, reduce the heat to low, and gently simmer until the beans are creamy, tender, and cooked through, about 2 hours. If the contents of the pot begin to look dry, add more water as needed.

Add the olives to the stew. Working in batches, add the kale, allowing each addition to wilt before adding more. Simmer until the kale is tender, about 12 minutes. If the stew is too thick, add more water to reach the desired consistency. Season with more salt or lemon juice, if needed. Remove and discard the bay leaves. Divide the stew among shallow bowls, top with feta, and serve immediately.

PAPPARDELLE WITH GREEN OLIVES AND BURRATA

Serves 4 to 6 as a main course

This rich pasta, coated with green olives and garlic sautéed in butter, is simple to prepare. Lemon adds acidity for balance, while the burrata and the warm pappardelle create a creamy finish.

INGREDIENTS

½ teaspoon kosher salt, plus more for pasta cooking water

1 pound dried pappardelle pasta

2 tablespoons unsalted butter

1 tablespoon extra-virgin olive oil, plus more for drizzling

1½ cups Castelvetrano olives, pitted

4 cloves garlic, minced

2 tablespoons freshly squeezed lemon juice

Freshly ground black pepper to taste

8 ounces burrata cheese, torn

¼ cup grated pecorino

Fresh thyme sprigs for garnish

Bring a pot of water to a boil and salt it to taste. Cook the pasta according to package instructions until al dente. Drain, reserving 1 cup of the pasta cooking water.

Meanwhile, in a large skillet heat the butter and 1 tablespoon oil over medium heat. Add the olives and garlic and cook, stirring occasionally, until the garlic is softened and fragrant, 2 to 3 minutes. Stir in the lemon juice.

Add the pasta and the reserved pasta cooking water. Toss the olives and garlic with the pasta until the sauce has thickened and coats the pasta, 2 to 3 minutes.

Season with pepper. Add the ½ teaspoon salt and toss to combine. Divide the hot pasta among plates and top with the cheeses. Drizzle with oil, and thyme, and serve immediately.

PANKO

IN MY OPINION, a hot bubbling gratin with a crispy panko breadcrumb topping is far superior to one with an old-fashioned breadcrumb topping. What sets this pantry staple apart from other breadcrumbs is its flaky texture as well as how it is prepared. Made from crustless white bread, panko is baked using an electrical current instead of heat, as in a traditional oven. This unique method was developed out of necessity when Japanese soldiers did not have access to traditional ovens for baking during World War II.

Flakier in consistency than standard breadcrumbs, panko lends a light crunchiness to dishes. On its own panko has little to no flavor, so it takes on the taste of any food it is paired with. This beguiling breadcrumb can be used in almost any recipe that calls for breadcrumbs and adds a textural dimension to mac and cheese, vegetable gratin, Scotch eggs, and meatballs. If a recipe calls for fine breadcrumbs, pulse panko in a food processor or break it up with your hands to achieve the desired result.

PANKO POSSIBILITIES

Baked scallops topped with panko wear a gorgeous golden-brown crust. For a delightful dinner, serve the scallops with a lemon-butter sauce and a green salad.

Salmon encrusted with panko, rosemary, and walnuts is not only delectable but provides a super source of omega-3 fatty acids. Pair the salmon with roasted potatoes or your grain of choice.

For a healthy take on the traditional chicken pot pie, make a panko, cauliflower, and cheddar cheese crust. Sitting atop layers of sautéed vegetables and tender chicken, the topping turns golden brown in the oven.

Reminiscent of fried chicken, buttermilk fried tofu is a tasty twist on an old favorite. Dip the tofu in buttermilk, then dredge in seasoned panko breadcrumbs for a crunchy coating.

Panko-crusted lobster cakes make a decadent dinner. Drizzle browned butter on the succulent cakes.

Lemon-scented panko topping adds a wonderful zingy crunch to a roasted Brussels sprouts gratin with a classic Parmesan mornay sauce.

For a glorious appetizer of stuffed mushrooms, add a little dry sherry, Gruyère cheese, and sautéed garlic to the panko stuffing.

BAKED TOMATOES WITH A PARMESAN, HERB, AND PANKO CRUST

Serves 4 to 6 as a light main course or side dish

Baked tomatoes atop a bed of arugula are a favorite summertime lunch. This easy dish is also great served with grilled chicken for dinner.

INGREDIENTS

6 ripe tomatoes

1 cup panko breadcrumbs

¼ cup grated Parmigiano Reggiano

1 tablespoon plus 1½ teaspoons minced flat-leaf parsley

1 tablespoon minced fresh thyme

1 clove garlic, minced

1 teaspoon kosher salt

½ teaspoon freshly ground black pepper

4 tablespoons unsalted butter, melted

2 tablespoons honey

3 tablespoons balsamic vinegar

One 5-ounce bag baby arugula

Preheat the oven to 375°F. Line a baking sheet with parchment paper and set aside.

Halve the tomatoes lengthwise. Gently scoop out the seeds from the tomato halves and set the tomato halves aside. Discard the seeds.

Combine the panko, Parmigiano, parsley, thyme, garlic, salt, and pepper in a small bowl and toss. Add the melted butter and stir until the mixture is completely coated in butter. Set aside.

In a separate bowl, whisk together the honey and vinegar.

Dip the cut side of a tomato half in the honey-vinegar mixture and then in the panko mixture. Place the coated side up on the prepared baking sheet. Repeat with the remaining tomato halves.

Bake in the preheated oven until the tomatoes are soft and the topping is golden brown, 20 to 25 minutes. Allow the tomatoes to cool on the baking sheet for 5 minutes, then serve on a bed of arugala.

ROASTED TROUT WITH LEMON-HERB PANKO

Serves 4 as a main course

This trout is an ideal weeknight dinner. The thin, tender filets cook in minutes, while the panko mixture with lemon and sumac imparts freshness and a savory crunch. Serve with a side salad of mixed herbs dressed with a blue cheese vinigrette, chopped almonds, and a buttery white wine.

INGREDIENTS

2 tablespoons toasted sesame seeds

2 tablespoons fresh thyme leaves

2 teaspoons sumac

I teaspoon finely grated lemon zest

I teaspoon kosher salt

½ teaspoon freshly ground black pepper

I cup panko breadcrumbs

4 tablespoons unsalted butter, melted

Four 6-ounce trout filets with skin

Preheat the oven to 425°F. Line a baking sheet with parchment paper and set aside.

In a medium bowl, combine the sesame seeds, thyme, sumac, lemon zest, ½ teaspoon of the salt, and ¼ teaspoon of the pepper. Stir in the panko and butter until well combined.

Season the trout with the remaining ½ teaspoon salt and ¼ teaspoon pepper. Place the fish on the prepared baking sheet, skin-side down. Spoon the seasoned panko evenly over the fish.

Roast in the preheated oven until the fish is opaque and the seasoned panko is golden, 10 to 12 minutes. Serve immediately.

SHEET-PAN PANKO LAMB MEATBALLS WITH WALNUT CHIMICHURRI SAUCE

Serves 4 as a main course or as a starter

These easy oven-roasted lamb meatballs with an herb-flavored sauce are a weeknight family favorite. They are also perfect as bite-size party food. Use this recipe as a template for endless creations. Try different spices, meats, and herbs to find a flavor that satisfies any palate.

INGREDIENTS

1 cup finely chopped
  flat-leaf parsley
½ cup finely chopped cilantro
½ cup finely chopped fresh mint
Juice and finely grated zest
  of 1 small lemon

2 tablespoons capers, rinsed,
  drained, and finely chopped
½ cup finely chopped walnuts
3 cloves garlic
½ cup extra-virgin olive oil
2 teaspoons kosher salt
2 teaspoons freshly ground
  black pepper

1 large egg
1 tablespoon sweet paprika
½ tablespoon hot paprika
¼ teaspoon ground cayenne pepper
1 cup panko breadcrumbs
1½ pounds ground lamb

Preheat the oven to 425°F.

In a medium bowl, combine the parsley, cilantro, and mint. Transfer half of the chopped herb mixture to a small bowl. To the small bowl, add the lemon zest, lemon juice, about half of the capers, and about half of the walnuts.

With a microplane grate 1 garlic clove into the small bowl. Thoroughly whisk in ¼ cup plus 1 tablespoon of the oil. Season with ½ teaspoon of the salt and ½ teaspoon of the pepper. Set the chimichurri sauce aside.

Combine the remaining capers and walnuts with the herb mixture in the medium bowl. With a microplane, grate the remaining 2 garlic cloves into the bowl. Whisk in the egg, paprika, cayenne, 1½ teaspoons salt, remaining 1½ teaspoons black pepper, and 1 tablespoon of the oil.

Mix the panko into the egg mixture. Add the ground lamb and gently knead the mixture by hand to combine. Be careful not to overmix. Brush the remaining 2 tablespoons oil onto a baking sheet. Pull off pieces of the meat mixture and roll into meatballs, each about the size of a golf ball. Place each ball at least 1 inch apart on the prepared pan.

Bake the meatballs in the preheated oven for 10 to 15 minutes, shaking the pan halfway through baking. Continue to bake until they are crispy on all sides.

Remove from the oven and transfer to a serving platter. Drizzle the meatballs with some of the walnut chimichurri sauce and serve the remaining sauce on the side.

PINE NUTS

WHETHER PINE NUTS ARE USED IN A SWEET OR SAVORY RECIPE, their enticing flavor complements an array of foods. From a classic pesto to traditional Italian Christmas cookies, their nutty taste is unmistakable. Pine nuts also pair well with anchovies, basil, cinnamon, citrus fruits, clove, ginger, grains, nutmeg, olives, oregano, raisins, rosemary, saffron, sardines, and thyme.

Pine nuts are sometimes labeled piñones (their Spanish name) or pinoli (Italian). They are actually not nuts but are the edible seeds of pine cones. Due to their slow growth and labor-intensive harvesting process, the little seeds are one of the most expensive nuts on the market. However, they are worth the cost as it takes only a small amount to add incredible flavor to any dish. And while they are delicious raw, toasting them brings out their immensely nutty flavor.

TOASTING PINE NUTS

The methods for toasting pine nuts are on the stovetop in a skillet or on a baking sheet in the oven. Either of these simple methods quickly brings out their natural aroma and enhances their flavor.

Skillet method: For a small amount, I opt to dry-roast the seeds on the stove. Place the pine nuts in a skillet and cook them over medium-low heat, stirring frequently, until golden and fragrant, about 3 minutes. This is a very quick and convenient method; however, the nuts can burn in an instant.

Oven method: Spread the nuts on a baking sheet and bake at 375°F, stirring occasionally, until they are golden brown, 4 to 5 minutes. This method will give you a more evenly toasted nut. You can also use a toaster oven for a small amount.

PINE NUT STORAGE

Due to their high oil content, pine nuts turn rancid quickly if not properly stored. Once rancid, they give off an unpleasant odor and often develop a bitter taste. Pine nuts should be kept in an airtight container in the refrigerator, where they will last up to two months. To extend the shelf life of pine nuts, place them in a heavy-duty freezer bag in the freezer. There they will last up to six months.

TOASTED GARLIC PESTO

Makes 1 cup

Homemade pesto is one of the best ways to enjoy a bounty of fresh basil. I like to toast the garlic with skins on in the same skillet as the pine nuts. The heat mellows the garlic's flavor. This basil-laden pesto can be used in many ways. Stir a scoop into soup or mix it in a pasta dish to add a fresh burst of flavor. Spread it on toasted bread or use it as a pizza base or sandwich spread. Pesto is also a great dip for roasted vegetables.

INGREDIENTS

⅓ cup pine nuts

3 cloves garlic, unpeeled

2 packed cups fresh basil leaves

½ cup grated Parmigiano Reggiano

½ teaspoon kosher salt

¼ teaspoon freshly ground black pepper

½ cup extra-virgin olive oil

Place the pine nuts and garlic in a skillet. Cook over medium-low heat, stirring frequently, until the pine nuts are golden and the color of the garlic deepens slightly, 3 to 5 minutes. Remove from the heat. Allow the garlic to cool, then peel and coarsely chop.

Place the pine nuts and the basil leaves in the bowl of a food processor fitted with the metal blade and pulse 8 to 10 times. Add the garlic and Parmigiano and pulse until the basil and pine nuts are fully chopped and form a paste. Scrape down the sides of the food processor with a rubber spatula.

Add the salt and pepper. With the food processor running, add the oil through the tube in a thin, steady stream. Adding the oil slowly while the processor is running keeps it from separating. Scrape down the sides of the food processor, if needed.

Transfer the pesto to a small bowl. Basil pesto will darken when it is exposed to air, so cover the bowl of pesto tightly with plastic wrap, making certain that the wrap is resting on the surface of the pesto, and refrigerate immediately. Stored in an airtight container, the pesto will last up to five days in the refrigerator.

TOASTED PINE NUT AND ROASTED SHALLOT TARTE TATIN

Makes one 10-inch tart, 4 to 6 servings

This savory tart is an amalgamation of a *BBC Good Food* recipe and my longtime favorite from the restaurant 8 Hoxton Square in London, now sadly closed. Do not be put off by the large amount of shallots. Once roasted, they become sweet and tender.

INGREDIENTS

3 tablespoons pine nuts

8 large shallots, peeled and halved lengthwise

2 teaspoons extra-virgin olive oil, plus more for drizzling

Kosher salt to taste

Freshly ground black pepper to taste

¼ cup balsamic vinegar

1 tablespoon white balsamic vinegar

1 teaspoon light brown sugar

3 tablespoons unsalted butter

One 17.3-ounce package frozen puff pastry, thawed

Unbleached all-purpose flour for work surface

½ cup sliced cremini mushrooms

½ cup sliced shiitake mushrooms

1 clove garlic, crushed

4 ounces burrata, torn into small pieces

½ cup baby arugula

½ ounce Parmigiano Reggiano, grated

Preheat the oven to 350°F.

Place the pine nuts on a rimmed baking sheet and toast them in the oven until they are golden brown, about 4 minutes. Transfer the pine nuts to a small bowl, and raise the oven temperature to 400°F.

On the same baking sheet, toss the shallots with the 2 teaspoons olive oil and season with salt and pepper to taste. Roast the shallots until they are tender and lightly browned, 20 to 25 minutes. Set the baking sheet aside and allow the shallots to cool.

In a 10-inch skillet bring the vinegars and brown sugar to a simmer over medium-low heat and cook until syrupy, about 5 minutes. Stir in 1 tablespoon of the butter and remove from the heat. Arrange the shallots cut-side up in the skillet, overlapping slightly to fill in any gaps.

Stack the puff pastry (which will be in two sheets) on a lightly floured surface. Gently roll the two sheets until they adhere to one another. Then roll out the pastry 1 inch larger in diameter than the skillet. Prick the pastry several times with a fork. Drape the pastry over

the shallots and carefully tuck the edges inside the skillet.

Bake the tart until the pastry is golden brown and puffed, 25 to 30 minutes.

While the tart is baking, melt the remaining 2 tablespoons butter in a skillet over medium-high heat. Sauté the mushrooms and garlic until the mushrooms are tender and brown, about 5 minutes. Season with salt and pepper to taste and set aside.

Once the tart is removed from the oven, allow it to sit until the pastry has cooled slightly, 5 to 8 minutes. Carefully invert the tart onto a plate and lift off the skillet. Top the tart with the burrata, sautéed mushrooms, arugula, Parmigiano Reggiano, and pine nuts. Drizzle with olive oil and serve.

CRAB AND PINE NUT LASAGNA

Serves 8 to 10 as a main course

Layers of pasta, Parmigiano Reggiano, pecorino Romano, and lump crab topped with a creamy béchamel sauce offer a decadent backdrop for pine nuts.

INGREDIENTS

1 teaspoon kosher salt, plus more for pasta cooking water

1 pound dried lasagna (do not use the no-boil type)

4 cups whole milk

1 stick (8 tablespoons) unsalted butter, plus more for pan

3 cloves garlic, minced

¼ cup unbleached all-purpose flour, sifted

Grated zest of 1 lemon

8 ounces lump crabmeat

½ cup grated Parmigiano Reggiano

½ cup grated pecorino Romano

8 ounces cremini mushrooms, stemmed and thinly sliced

½ cup whole milk ricotta

¾ cup pine nuts

Fresh thyme sprigs for garnish

Bring a large pot of water to a boil and salt it to taste. Add the pasta and cook at a high simmer until al dente, 6 to 8 minutes. Drain well and set aside.

In a small saucepan, heat the milk until it just begins to bubble. In a medium saucepan, melt 1 stick butter over medium-low heat. Add the garlic and sauté for 2 minutes. Add the flour and continue stirring for 1 minute. Whisk in the hot milk. Continue to cook over medium-low heat, whisking constantly, until the mixture is as thick as heavy cream, 25 to 30 minutes. Stir in the lemon zest and the 1 teaspoon salt. Remove the saucepan from the heat.

Meanwhile, preheat the oven to 375°F.

Grease a 9 by 13-inch baking dish with butter. Layer the pasta in the bottom of the dish with the sides of the noodles touching so there are no gaps. Top the pasta with the crabmeat, one third of the sauce, and half of the grated cheeses.

Top with another layer of pasta and add the mushrooms. Place dollops of ricotta on the mushrooms and drizzle one-third of the remaining sauce. Add the final layer of pasta and the remaining sauce. Cover the top layer with the remaining grated cheese and sprinkle on the pine nuts. Bake in the oven until bubbling and golden brown, about 30 minutes. Let the lasagna rest for about 10 minutes. Garnish with thyme and serve.

ITALIAN PIGNOLI COOKIES

Makes 24 cookies

Pignoli cookies are a treasured Italian Christmas dessert that are chewy and require only five ingredients. The pine nuts and almond paste impart a fabulous flavor. For a true treat, serve the cookies with a cup of coffee or espresso. Note that you must use almond paste, not marzipan. The dough is sticky, so line the baking sheets with parchment.

INGREDIENTS

1 pound almond paste
1 cup sugar
2 egg whites, room temperature
2 teaspoons grated orange zest
1¼ cups pine nuts

Preheat the oven to 350°F. Line two baking sheets with parchment paper and set aside.

Place the almond paste in the bowl of a food processor fitted with the metal blade. Pulse a few times until the paste forms small crumbs. Add the sugar and pulse a few more times, until the almond paste resembles cornmeal.

Add the egg whites and the orange zest to the bowl. Process until the dough is smooth, about 30 seconds. Turn the dough onto a wooden surface.

Pour the pine nuts into a large bowl. Roll 1 tablespoon of the dough into a small ball. Repeat with the remaining dough. Gently drop a ball of dough into the pine nuts and coat the top surface. Place on one of the prepared baking sheets. Repeat with the remaining dough and pine nuts, positioning the cookies 2 inches apart. Bake until lightly browned, 13 to 15 minutes.

Cool the cookies on the baking sheets on a rack for 5 minutes, then use a spatula to transfer them directly to the rack to finish cooling.

POLENTA

LIKE MAKING RISOTTO, making polenta has a reputation for being laborious. Traditional Italian cooks still prepare polenta in unlined copper pots, while some Italian grandmothers still insist on cooking the corn porridge over a wood fire in a hearth while stirring nonstop. Thankfully polenta is not difficult to make and is very forgiving.

Polenta, which originated as a peasant food in Northern Italy, is frequently eaten with meats, ragù, and cheeses. Delicious as a dinner straight out of the pot with a pat of butter and a handful of grated Parmigiano Reggiano, it is also a wonderful hot cereal with milk or topped with an egg.

Soft polenta can be poured into flat pans and, once firm, cut into slices. The thin slices can be grilled, fried, sautéed, or layered with tomato sauce and baked like a lasagna. For appetizers, you can top polenta slices with sautéed mushrooms, pesto, tapenade, or prosciutto.

POLENTA, CORNMEAL, AND GRITS

Polenta is both an ingredient and a dish. With its deep yellow color, polenta is made from cornmeal derived from stoneground eight-row flint corn, or otto file in Italian. Grits are similar but traditionally prepared using white field corn or dent corn. Lighter in color, grits contain more starch than polenta. Though both are available in a variety of grinds, polenta is typically coarser than grits.

MAKING POLENTA

There is no getting around the fact that you need 30 to 40 minutes to make a traditional polenta. That said, it is really very easy. The trick is to allow sufficient cooking time for the cornmeal to swell and release its sweet natural flavor.

Compared to other grains, polenta requires a lot of water. The ratio is usually 4 parts cold water to 1 part polenta. Bring a large pot of water to a rapid boil and slowly pour in the cornmeal, whisking for 3 to 5 minutes. Once it thickens, turn the heat down very low and allow the polenta to bubble gently.

The idea of constant stirring is largely a romantic one, and despite the advice of some devotees, I stir my polenta about every 5 minutes. The most important thing is to check that it is cooking evenly. If polenta gets too thick, it will not cook properly. If needed, you can stir in a little more water or broth.

FUN FACT: The kind of pot that you use for cooking polenta makes a big difference. A heavy-gauge copper pot called a paiolo is traditionally used in Italy to make polenta. The flared sides facilitate easy stirring and steady water absorption, ensuring a creamy texture. If you do not have a copper polenta pot, use an enameled cast iron or other heavy pot to keep the polenta from sticking and scorching.

RUSTIC PARMESAN AND POLENTA CHICKEN SOUP

Serves 4 to 6 as a main course

I adore this easy-to-prepare soup with spinach and chicken. It is wonderful paired with a rustic bread and a crisp white wine.

INGREDIENTS

1 tablespoon extra-virgin olive oil, plus more for drizzling

1 shallot, diced

2 medium cloves garlic, minced

6 cups chicken stock

½ cup stoneground yellow cornmeal

1 cup grated Parmigiano Reggiano

8 ounces baby spinach leaves

2 cups shredded rotisserie chicken

½ teaspoon kosher salt

½ teaspoon coarsely ground black pepper

Heat 1 tablespoon oil in a large stockpot over medium heat. Add the shallot and garlic. Sauté for 3 minutes until tender.

Add the stock to the pot and bring it to a simmer. Add the cornmeal to the stock in a thin stream, whisking constantly. Simmer over medium heat, stirring occasionally, until the soup is slightly thickened, about 10 minutes.

Whisk in the cheese and simmer for 1 additional minute. Stir in the spinach and chicken. Simmer until the spinach is wilted and the chicken is heated through, 3 to 5 minutes.

Season the soup with salt and pepper. Ladle into bowls and drizzle with olive oil.

POLENTA AND PORK RAGÙ

Serves 6 to 8 as a main course

Savory pork with creamy polenta that absorbs the juices of the meat is pure comfort food. Enjoy a warm bowl and a glass of Chianti in front of a roaring fire with friends.

INGREDIENTS

3 pounds skinless, boneless pork shoulder, cut into 3 pieces

1 tablespoon plus 1½ teaspoons kosher salt

2½ teaspoons freshly ground pepper

1 tablespoon extra-virgin olive oil

3 large shallots, finely diced

8 cloves garlic, minced

1 tablespoon tomato paste

½ cup Chianti wine

One 28-ounce can whole peeled tomatoes, preferably Mutti

Leaves of 6 sprigs fresh thyme

2 bay leaves

1½ cups stoneground yellow cornmeal

4 tablespoons unsalted butter

½ cup grated Parmigiano Reggiano, plus more for garnish

Season the pork with 2 teaspoons salt and 1 teaspoon pepper. Heat the oil in a large heavy pot over medium heat. Cook the pork, turning often, until it is evenly browned, 10 to 12 minutes. Once browned, transfer it to a platter and pour off the pan drippings.

Add the shallots and garlic to the pot and cook, stirring occasionally, until tender, 2 to 5 minutes. Add the tomato paste and cook for 5 minutes.

Add the wine and cook, scraping up any browned bits, until it is reduced by half, about 5 minutes. Add the tomatoes, thyme, and bay leaves. Break the tomatoes with a wooden spoon. Stir in 2 cups water and return the pork with any accumulated juices to the pot. Season with 1 teaspoon salt and 1 teaspoon pepper.

Bring the liquid to a boil, then reduce the heat to simmer on medium-low. Partially cover the pot and cook until the pork is tender, about 3 hours. Shred the pork in the pot.

In another large pot, bring 6 cups water and 1 teaspoon salt to a boil over high heat. Whisking constantly, add the cornmeal in a thin stream. Reduce the heat to medium-low. Cook the cornmeal, whisking often, until it is creamy, about 25 minutes. Add the butter and the Parmigiano and whisk until melted. Season with the remaining ½ teaspoon salt and ½ teaspoon pepper. Spoon the polenta into bowls and top with pork ragù and Parmigiano.

LEMON POLENTA CAKE

Makes one 8-inch round cake, about 8 servings

This rustic Italian-style cake, made with stoneground cornmeal and lots of fresh lemon, is delicious on its own or drizzled with olive oil. Dust the cake with powdered sugar and serve it with fresh berries.

INGREDIENTS

Cooking spray for pan

1 cup stoneground yellow cornmeal

¾ cup unbleached all-purpose flour

1½ teaspoons baking powder

½ teaspoon sea salt

2 large eggs, room temperature

2 egg whites

1 cup granulated sugar

¼ cup grapeseed oil

2 tablespoons unsalted butter, softened

½ cup sour cream

1 tablespoon grated lemon zest

3 tablespoons freshly squeezed lemon juice

¼ cup powdered sugar

Preheat the oven to 350°F.

Line the bottom of an 8-inch round cake pan with parchment paper. Lightly coat the sides of the pan with cooking spray.

Whisk the cornmeal, flour, baking powder, and salt in a bowl and set aside.

In a large bowl, beat the eggs, egg whites, and sugar with a mixer on medium-high speed until pale and creamy, about 5 minutes. On low speed, mix in the oil, butter, sour cream, and lemon zest and juice. Stir in the dry ingredients with a spoon until just blended.

Pour the batter into the prepared pan and bake until the top feels firm and a toothpick inserted in the center of the cake comes out clean, 35 to 40 minutes. Cool the cake in the pan for 10 minutes, then run a dull knife around the edge of the pan to loosen it. Invert it onto a rack to cool completely. Sift the powdered sugar over the cake just before serving.

PRUNES

RICH GUINNESS STEW, cinnamon-scented Moroccan lamb tagine, and a rustic apple-laden pork tenderloin all share a crucial ingredient—prunes. With a lovely mellow sweetness, prunes add texture, depth, and substance to both sweet and savory recipes, which makes them a standard pantry staple in many regions of the world. Prunes pair perfectly with a wide array of foods and beverages, from dark chocolate mousse to craft beer, and can take a dish from average to awesome. For Thanksgiving I like to surprise my guests with a savory stuffing adorned with chestnuts, bacon, and prunes.

Sadly, for some prunes bring memories of murky glasses of juice they drank as children. Personally, I have always loved prunes as a snack. However, I was a holdout on cooking with the dried fruit—my mistake. After years of hearing rave reviews, I finally made prune-studded chicken Marbella. First published in the legendary *The Silver Palate Cookbook*, the dish was the dinner party darling of the 1980s and famously called for olives, capers, and, yes, prunes. The briny-sweet combination was a hit, and it entirely changed my opinion.

POPULAR PRUNE DISHES AROUND THE WORLD
From prunes stuffed with blue cheese to white pepper crème brûlée with prune compote, France has a vast repertory of prune recipes. In fact, prunes enjoy the same prestige as foie gras among the French. And, in Lafitte-sur-Lot, a township in southwestern France, you will find the Musée du Pruneau, an entire museum dedicated to the fruit.

However, France is not the only country that has a love affair with the dried fruit. In Poland, Russia, and Ukraine, prunes covered in chocolate are a traditional confection.

Vínarterta, a flavorful, seven-layer Icelandic cake, features prune jam infused with cardamom, cinnamon, and cloves between thin layers of almond dough.

Far breton is a classic dessert from the Brittany region of France. A rich custard made with prunes soaked in Armagnac, brandy, or rum, it is delicious served with a warm cup of coffee.

In Eastern Europe, especially Georgia, kharcho reigns supreme. In this hearty soup, beef is bathed in a tomato broth and smothered with fresh herbs, alongside rice, walnuts, and prunes.

For a knockout wintertime supper, British food writer Diana Henry makes pork sausages with prunes. The baked sausages, topped with a sauce of red wine, crème de cassis, and onions, are served with an orange zest, garlic, and walnut gremolata.

Bigos is an Eastern European stew with many variations. Also known as hunter's stew, it is the national dish of Poland. An assortment of chopped meat is stewed with sauerkraut, shredded cabbage, prunes, and wine. This dish is even more delicious when it is sopped up with crusty bread.

SCOTTISH COCK-A-LEEKIE SOUP

Serves 4 as a main course

Cock-a-leekie is a delicious soup with a funny name. Consisting mainly of chicken (cock) and leeks (leekie), it is Scotland's national soup. The earliest reference to the bowl of broth was in 1598—the English author Fynes Moryson wrote that he had been served "pullet with some prunes in the broth" at a knight's house in Scotland. Though this is traditionally made with stewed chicken, I opt for rotisserie chicken to make a quick and easy meal.

INGREDIENTS

1½ teaspoons extra-virgin olive oil

1 tablespoon salted butter

4 carrots, sliced on the diagonal

2 ribs celery, diced

8 leeks, white and pale green parts sliced

1 shallot, thinly sliced

1 teaspoon kosher salt

⅛ teaspoon freshly ground white pepper

¼ cup dry white wine

6 cups chicken stock

2 cups shredded rotisserie chicken

2 bay leaves

4 sprigs fresh thyme, plus more for garnish

12 pitted prunes

In a large stockpot, warm the oil and butter over medium-low heat. Add the carrots, celery, leeks, and shallot. Sauté until the vegetables are tender, about 20 minutes. Stir in the salt, pepper, and wine.

Pour the stock into the pot and stir to combine, then add the chicken, bay leaves, thyme, and prunes.

Bring to a boil, then lower the heat to a gentle simmer. Cover and cook for 25 minutes. Discard the bay leaves and thyme sprigs. Garnish with fresh thyme and serve hot.

RUSTIC FRENCH PORK WITH PRUNES AND APPLES

Serves 6 as a main course

This easy dish is succulent and savory. Onions, apples, and prunes nestled underneath a roasted pork loin provide incredible flavor. The pork, spiked with herbes de Provence, a combination of thyme, basil, savory, and lavender, permeates the kitchen. Note that you cannot substitute the pork tenderloin for the pork loin in this recipe. The smaller cut of meat has very little marbling and cooks in less time.

INGREDIENTS

One 3-pound boneless pork loin roast
1 tablespoon kosher salt
2 tablespoons olive oil
2 tablespoons unsalted butter
2 large yellow onions, thinly sliced
½ cup apple cider vinegar

½ cup beef broth
3 Granny Smith apples, cored and quartered
1 cup pitted prunes
1 tablespoon herbes de Provence
2 teaspoons freshly ground coarse black pepper

Move a rack to the middle of the oven and preheat to 400°F.

Pat the pork loin dry with paper towels and evenly sprinkle with the salt. In a large cast-iron pan or skillet, heat the oil over medium-high. Add the pork and sear it on all sides until it is a deep golden-brown, 4 to 6 minutes per side. Once all sides are seared, transfer the pork to a platter.

Add the butter and the onions to the same pan and sauté for 3 minutes. Add ¼ cup of the vinegar and ¼ cup of the broth, scraping up any browned bits. Add the apples, prunes, and herbes de Provence and remove from the heat.

In a roasting pan nestle the pork loin, any accumulated juices, and the prune mixture. Pour the remaining ¼ cup vinegar and ¼ cup broth over the pork and sprinkle with the pepper. Roast the pork in the preheated oven until an instant-read thermometer inserted into the thickest part of the meat reads 145°F, about 1 hour.

Remove the pan from the oven and transfer the pork to a clean cutting board. Let it rest for 20 minutes. Slice the pork and serve it on a platter with the onions, apples, prunes, and pan drippings.

MODERN CHICKEN MARBELLA

Serves 6 to 8 as a main course

Chicken Marbella is an iconic chicken dish from Sheila Lukins and Julee Rosso's *The Silver Palate Cookbook*, first published in 1982. The recipe is a careful balance of sweetness, acidity, and saltiness. This is my delicious, modern take on the beloved classic.

INGREDIENTS

½ cup walnut oil

½ cup red wine vinegar

1 cup pitted prunes

½ cup pitted Castelvetrano olives

¼ cup caperberries

½ cup capers with their brine

6 bay leaves

1 head garlic, peeled

¼ cup chopped fresh oregano, plus sprigs for garnish

2 teaspoons kosher salt

¼ teaspoon freshly ground black pepper

4 bone-in skin-on chicken breasts

4 bone-in skin-on chicken thighs

½ cup brown sugar

1 cup dry white wine

¼ cup dry sherry

In a large bowl, combine the oil, vinegar, prunes, olives, caperberries, capers and brine, bay leaves, garlic, oregano, salt, and pepper. Add the chicken pieces and turn to coat. Cover and refrigerate for 8 hours.

Preheat the oven to 375°F. Arrange the chicken in a single layer in a shallow roasting pan and spoon the marinade evenly over it. Sprinkle with the brown sugar and pour the wine and sherry into the pan.

Bake until the thigh pieces yield clear juice when pricked with a fork or the chicken reaches 145°F on an instant-read thermometer, 50 to 60 minutes.

Remove the pan from the oven, cover tightly with aluminum foil, and allow to rest for 10 to 15 minutes. Remove and discard the bay leaves. Transfer the chicken pieces to a warm serving platter and top with the prunes, olives, caperberries, capers, and garlic; keep warm. Reserve the pan juices.

Garnish the chicken with the oregano. Place the roasting pan over medium heat and bring the pan juices to a boil. Reduce to about ½ cup. Strain into a heatproof bowl and serve the sauce alongside the chicken.

DAUBE À LA PROVENÇAL

Serves 4 to 6 as a main course

This slow-cooked stew with hints of citrus, is Provence's answer to beef bourguignon. My version was inspired by Julia Child's recipe, which she made often at her home in Provence.

INGREDIENTS

3 pounds beef chuck shoulder roast,
  cut into 2-inch pieces

3 cups red wine, such as Côtes du Rhône

¼ cup cognac or brandy

3 cloves garlic, crushed

3 bay leaves

3 tablespoons extra-virgin olive oil

2 teaspoons kosher salt

1 teaspoon freshly ground black pepper

1 medium yellow onion, diced

3 carrots, shredded

One 16-ounce can diced tomatoes,
  preferably Mutti

1 teaspoon sweet paprika

1 cinnamon stick

1 tablespoon brown sugar

1 cup pitted prunes

1 tablespoon sherry vinegar

2 tablespoons freshly squeezed orange juice

4 sprigs fresh thyme

Finely chopped flat-leaf parsley for garnish

Place the beef in a large non-reactive bowl. Add the wine, cognac, garlic, and bay leaves and toss to coat. Cover and marinate in the refrigerator for at least 3 hours, stirring occasionally.

Preheat the oven to 300°F.

Lift the beef out of the marinade with a slotted spoon. Pat the beef dry with paper towels and transfer to a large platter. Reserve the marinade. Heat 2 tablespoons of the oil in a Dutch oven over medium-high heat. Add the beef and season with 1 teaspoon salt and ½ teaspoon pepper. Thoroughly brown the beef cubes on all sides. Once the meat is browned, transfer it back to the platter and set aside.

Add the onion and the remaining 1 tablespoon oil to the pot. Sauté until soft, stirring occasionally, about 5 minutes. Pour the reserved marinade into the pot and scrape up any browned bits. Add the carrots, tomatoes, paprika, cinnamon stick, sugar, prunes, vinegar, orange juice, and thyme, and the remaining 1 teaspoon salt and ½ teaspoon pepper. Bring to a boil, then reduce the heat and simmer for 5 minutes. Return the beef to the pot. Cover and bake in the preheated oven until the beef is tender, about 3 hours. Remove and discard the bay leaves, cinnamon stick, and thyme sprigs. Serve hot.

QUINOA

ONCE FOUND ONLY ON THE SHELVES OF HEALTH FOOD STORES, quinoa has become phenomenally popular in recent decades. Now gracing the aisles of national supermarket chains, it is a favored food in the United States. However, its history goes way back. Often called the gold of the Incas, it has been cultivated in the Andes for over five thousand years. Technically a seed, quinoa is treated as a grain. A complete protein with nine essential amino acids, and high in iron, magnesium, and fiber, quinoa is a healthy pantry staple that is incredibly versatile and easy to cook.

Quinoa makes a great side dish when simply cooked in broth. I love to add it to soups and stews. It can also be used to make breakfast porridges and summer salads, or as a bed for poached chicken. I often make a pot on weekends to keep in the refrigerator and then pair it with grilled vegetables for lunches all week long.

Quinoa has a natural coating called saponin that can make the cooked grain taste bitter. To remove the coating simply rinse the quinoa under cold water just before cooking. Boxed quinoa is often pre-rinsed, but I still give the seeds an additional rinse.

Quinoa is very easy to prepare. Following is my foolproof basic recipe.

BASIC QUINOA
Makes 3 cups

1 cup quinoa
½ teaspoon extra-virgin olive oil
1¾ cups water or chicken or vegetable broth
½ teaspoon kosher salt

Rinse the quinoa in a fine-mesh strainer under cold running water and drain.

Heat the oil in a saucepan over medium-high heat. Add the quinoa and cook, stirring constantly, until the quinoa is toasted, 2 to 3 minutes.

Add the water or broth and the salt. Bring to a rolling boil, then turn the heat to low. Cover and cook for 15 minutes.

Remove the covered pot from the heat and let stand for 5 minutes. Uncover the pot and gently fluff the quinoa with a fork. If any liquid remains, return the pot to a low heat. Cover and cook until the remaining liquid is absorbed, then fluff again.

QUINOA DISHES TO TRY
Quinoa has a lovely nutty flavor and is a nice alternative to rice, couscous, or other grains. It is equally terrific as a cold salad, a warm side dish, or mixed with any kind of beans and roasted vegetables as a main course. From zesty chili to crispy sliders, here are ways to add quinoa to your diet.

For an aromatic gratin, combine quinoa, zucchini, rosemary, thyme, and Gruyère.

Quinoa and sautéed spinach topped with a soft poached egg is wonderful for lunch or dinner.

Chilled black quinoa tossed with tangy lemon zest, avocado, and salted pistachios makes a great summertime salad.

Kale and quinoa patties are scrumptious veggie burgers that are simple to make. Top with fresh pesto and goat cheese for a light dinner.

CURRIED QUINOA SALMON SALAD

Serves 2 to 4 as a light main course

With delicate salmon, crunchy kale, and a beautiful curry-scented soy dressing, this salad is a perfect combination of flavors and textures. Nutritious, easy to prepare, and delicious, it checks all the boxes and meets all my weeknight dinner requirements.

INGREDIENTS

Cooking spray for pan

1 tablespoon extra-virgin olive oil

2 tablespoons mild curry powder

2 tablespoons plus 1½ teaspoons freshly squeezed lemon juice

1 tablespoon fresh thyme leaves

1 tablespoon plus 1 teaspoon soy sauce or Bragg liquid aminos

1 pound salmon filet

1 tablespoon liquid coconut oil

1 teaspoon honey or agave nectar

2 cups cooked Basic Quinoa, cooled (see page 189)

2 cups finely chopped kale leaves

Preheat the oven to 350°F. Coat a 9 by 13-inch glass baking dish with cooking spray and set aside.

In a medium bowl, whisk together the olive oil, 1 tablespoon of the curry powder, 1½ teaspoons of the lemon juice, thyme, and 2 teaspoons of the soy sauce.

Place the salmon in the prepared baking dish skin side down. Pour the marinade over the salmon. Cover the baking dish with foil and refrigerate for 15 minutes.

Remove the salmon from the refrigerator. Bake in the preheated oven until the salmon is slightly firm to the touch, about 15 minutes. Remove the filet and allow to cool slightly.

In a large bowl, whisk together the coconut oil, remaining 1 tablespoon curry powder, remaining 2 tablespoons lemon juice, remaining 2 teaspoons soy sauce, and honey.

With a fork, fluff the quinoa and add it to the bowl with the dressing. Add the kale. Toss gently to coat the salad with the dressing. Remove the skin and lightly flake the cooled salmon with a fork and add it to the bowl. Toss to combine and serve.

APPLE AND AVOCADO QUINOA SALAD

Serves 4 to 6 as a light main course or side dish

This apple and quinoa salad, tossed with a delicious lemon Dijon dressing, is easy to make and perfect to serve as a side dish or for lunch. I love the crunchy texture and pops of sweetness from the fruit.

INGREDIENTS

3 cups cooked Basic Quinoa,
  at room temperature (see page 189)

2 ribs celery, sliced

2 scallions, white and pale green parts sliced

2 small Granny Smith apples, cored and sliced

½ cup roasted and salted pistachios,
  roughly chopped

⅓ cup dried cranberries

Kosher salt to taste

Freshly ground black pepper to taste

2 tablespoons apple cider vinegar

1 tablespoon honey

1 tablespoon grapeseed oil

2 teaspoons whole-grain mustard,
  preferably Maille

2 avocados, pitted, peeled, and sliced

Combine the quinoa, celery, scallions, apples, pistachios, and cranberries in a large serving bowl. Season with salt and pepper.

Whisk together the vinegar, honey, oil, and mustard in a small bowl. Pour the vinaigrette over the salad and toss to combine. Top with avocado slices and serve.

CASHEW-CREAM QUINOA SOUP

Serves 4 to 6 as a main course

With an excess of quinoa in the pantry and a jar of cashew cream in the refrigerator, I developed this wonderful quinoa soup. Inspired by a recipe I found on the website *Platings + Pairings*, the soup is hearty and perfect for wintertime.

INGREDIENTS

2 tablespoons extra-virgin olive oil

3 shallots, diced

4 carrots, shredded

I rib celery, diced

I teaspoon kosher salt

I teaspoon freshly ground black pepper

4 cloves garlic, minced

6 cups chicken or vegetable stock

One 15-ounce can chickpeas, drained and rinsed

I cup quinoa, rinsed

One 14.5-ounce can finely chopped tomatoes, preferably Mutti

I teaspoon dried basil

2 teaspoons dried thyme

½ teaspoon red pepper flakes

3 cups baby spinach

½ cup Cashew Cream (see below)

¼ cup grated Parmigiano Reggiano, for serving

CASHEW CREAM

Makes I cup

I cup raw cashews

2 tablespoons extra-virgin olive oil

2 tablespoons freshly squeezed lemon juice

I clove garlic

½ teaspoon sea salt

Heat the oil in a large stockpot or Dutch oven over medium-high. Add the shallots, carrots, and celery. Season with ½ teaspoon of the salt and ½ teaspoon of the pepper. Sauté, stirring occasionally, until soft, 5 to 7 minutes. Add the garlic and sauté for 1 minute.

Add the stock, chickpeas, quinoa, tomatoes, and spices. Stir to combine. Season with the remaining ½ teaspoon salt and the remaining ½ teaspoon pepper. Bring to a boil, then reduce the heat to a simmer. Partially cover the pot and cook for 25 minutes. Stir in the spinach and cashew cream. Allow the spinach to wilt. Divide among bowls and top with the grated cheese.

FOR THE CASHEW CREAM: Place the cashews and ½ cup water in a small bowl. Let sit in a warm area for at least 8 hours. Drain.

With a high-speed blender, blend the cashews, oil, lemon juice, garlic, and salt until smooth.

Store the cashew cream in an airtight container in the refrigerator for up to 1 week.

TURKEY QUINOA MEATLOAF

Serves 6 as a main course

My meatloaf-loving family initially thought this recipe was sacrilege. When they got a taste of its savory goodness, they quickly changed their tune. Based on a delicious version I found on the wonderful website *The Modern Proper*, it is a new family favorite. Thanks to the grated carrots, it is juicy and bursting with flavor. But the real secret is quinoa. It adds a wonderful texture and a nutty taste.

INGREDIENTS

⅓ cup quinoa, rinsed and drained
⅔ cup chicken stock
1 tablespoon extra-virgin olive oil
1 small yellow onion, finely diced
1 shallot, finely diced
1 large carrot, grated
4 cloves garlic, minced

2 pounds ground turkey
1 tablespoon tomato paste
¼ teaspoon ground cayenne pepper
1 teaspoon garlic powder
1 teaspoon onion powder
½ teaspoon sweet paprika

2 large eggs, lightly beaten
2 teaspoons kosher salt
1 teaspoon freshly ground black pepper
1 tablespoon light brown sugar
2 tablespoons Worcestershire sauce
Chopped flat-leaf parsley for garnish

Preheat the oven to 350°F. Line a baking sheet with parchment paper and set aside.

Bring the quinoa and stock to a boil in a saucepan over high heat. Reduce the heat to medium-low, cover, and simmer until the quinoa is tender and the liquid has been absorbed, 15 to 20 minutes. Set aside to cool.

Heat the oil in a skillet over medium heat. Stir in the onion, shallot, and carrot. Sauté until the onion is soft, about 5 minutes. Add the garlic and cook for 1 additional minute. Remove from the heat and allow to cool.

In a large bowl, place the turkey, quinoa, onion mixture, tomato paste, cayenne, garlic powder, onion powder, paprika, eggs, salt, and pepper. Use your hands to mix until combined. The mixture will be very moist. Shape into a loaf on the prepared baking sheet.

Combine the brown sugar and Worcestershire sauce in a small bowl. Brush over the top of the meatloaf. Bake in the preheated oven until the meatloaf is cooked through or an instant-read thermometer reads 160°F when inserted, 55 to 60 minutes. Allow the meatloaf to rest for 10 minutes before slicing. Garnish with parsley and serve.

R

RAISINS

PUT ASIDE THE MEMORIES OF A LITTLE CARDBOARD BOX at snack time during preschool—raisins are so much more. They are a pantry essential to be enjoyed on their own, and add an incredible fruity complexity to soups, salads, seafood, meat, poultry, and, of course, cookies. From a flavorful golden sauce for ham to a gravy for slow-roasted duck and warm winter salads, the options are plentiful. Try serving raisins infused with sherry alongside seared scallops or sprinkled over a poached fruit compote. Spirits and raisins are a great pairing, whether the raisins are soaked in sherry or plumped in whiskey. From black to red to golden and green, there are many types of raisins. The two varieties that I use most often are black and golden. Black, the most common, are sun-dried while golden are dried in a dehydrator.

GLOBAL CULINARY EXPRESSIONS

From India to Morocco to Italy or Greece, this sweet and succulent dried fruit adds a glorious global flavor to many recipes. Be inspired by the following traditional recipes, which vary from cook to cook and region to region.

Foriana is a sweet and savory sauce that is a staple on the island of Ischia, off the coast of Naples. A perfumed oil of garlic, oregano, nuts, and raisins, it is stirred it into stew, spooned over bruschetta, and traditionally tossed with pasta during Lent.

Mrouzia is a traditional Moroccan meat tagine, usually lamb, that is cooked in a syrupy sauce made of honey, onions, raisins, and almonds. Heavily scented with ginger, saffron, cumin, coriander, cinnamon, and cloves, it is served on special occasions, such as the Islamic holiday of Eid al-Adha, with couscous or crusty bread.

Pasta con le sarde is a classic dish in Sicily. Golden raisins and saffron are warmed and rehydrated in white wine to create a fragrant sauce of fennel, pine nuts, anchovies, and sardines. This flavorful sauce, influenced by the Arabs who once ruled Sicily, is served over bucatini or spaghetti topped with seasoned breadcrumbs.

Sehriyeli pilav is a fragrant Turkish pilaf that is a favorite for holiday feasts. Rice lightly spiced with cinnamon, cumin, and cardamom is tossed with pistachios, almonds, dried apricots, and raisins.

Shchi is a humble sweet and sour Russian cabbage soup. Served in a rich vegetable broth, it can include a variety of ingredients, among them carrots, turnips, bell peppers, tomatoes, prunes, and raisins.

RAISIN AND CARROT TART

Serves 4 as a light main course or side

This carrot tart is the perfect way to celebrate spring and summer. Serve it as a side or on its own as a delightful light lunch.

INGREDIENTS

Unbleached all-purpose flour for dusting surface

1 sheet (typically half of a 17.3-ounce package) frozen puff pastry, thawed

1 pound multicolored carrots, cut lengthwise into ¼-inch slices

1 tablespoon extra-virgin olive oil

1 teaspoon kosher salt, plus more to taste

1 teaspoon freshy ground black pepper, plus more to taste

2 cloves garlic

8 ounces ricotta

4 ounces feta, crumbled

½ cup golden raisins

Chopped fresh chives for garnish

Preheat the oven to 425°F with one rack on the top third and one on the bottom third. Line a baking sheet with parchment paper and set aside.

On a lightly floured surface, roll the puff pastry into a 10 by 14-inch rectangle. Using a paring knife, lightly score the border of the pastry to create a ¼-inch margin. Place the pastry on the prepared baking sheet and prick it inside the border with a fork to prevent puffing.

In a medium bowl, toss the carrots with the oil, 1 teaspoon salt, and 1 teaspoon pepper. Spread the carrots in a single layer on a separate baking sheet.

Place the puff pastry on the upper rack. Place the carrots on the lower rack. Bake the pastry until it is lightly golden, about 20 minutes. Remove from the oven and allow it to cool slightly. Roast the carrots until the edges are golden brown and the carrots are tender but crisp, 15 to 20 minutes.

While the puff pastry and carrots are in the oven, drop the garlic through the tube of a food processor fitted with the metal blade to mince. Add the ricotta, feta, and ¼ cup of the raisins and process until smooth. Season with salt and pepper. Spread the cheese mixture within the borders of the puff pastry. Sprinkle the remaining ¼ cup raisins over the cheese and arrange the carrots in a single layer on top.

Return to the oven and bake until the carrots are tender, and the edges of the cheese mixture start to turn golden brown, 15 to 20 minutes. Garnish with the chives, slice into squares, and serve.

GOLDEN CURRY CHICKEN SALAD WITH RAISINS

Serves 4 as a light main course

I love chicken salad. This recipe is an updated version of my childhood lunchtime favorite. Moist chicken tossed in creamy mayonnaise with crunchy celery, sweet raisins, salty cashews, and warm curry powder is my grown up go-to. It is wonderful on both toasted raisin bread or as a sandwich on slices of crusty French bread.

INGREDIENTS

2 whole bone-in skin-on chicken breasts
2 tablespoons extra-virgin olive oil
1½ teaspoons kosher salt
½ teaspoon freshly ground black pepper
¾ cup mayonnaise, preferably Duke's or Hellman's
3 tablespoons dry white wine
2 tablespoons curry powder

¼ teaspoon garam masala
¼ teaspoon ground turmeric
2 ribs celery, diced
¼ cup golden raisins
½ cup lightly salted whole cashews, chopped
Chopped flat-leaf parsley for garnish, optional

Preheat the oven to 350°F.

Brush the skin of the chicken with the oil and sprinkle with 1 teaspoon of the salt and the pepper.

Place the breasts in a roasting pan. Roast in the preheated oven until the chicken is cooked through, 45 to 50 minutes. Set aside until cool enough to handle. Discard the skin, remove the chicken from the bones, and dice the chicken.

In the bowl of a food processor fitted with a metal blade, combine the mayonnaise, wine, curry powder, garam masala, turmeric, and remaining ½ teaspoon salt. Process until smooth.

In a large bowl fold together the mayonnaise mixture and the diced chicken. Add the celery and raisins and mix well. Cover the chicken salad with plastic wrap and refrigerate for 1 hour.

Allow the chicken salad to come to room temperature, then mix in the cashews just before serving. Garnish with parsley, if desired.

SEARED SCALLOPS WITH SHERRY-INFUSED RAISINS

Serves 4 as a main course

The secret to golden pan-seared scallops is to cook them in piping hot butter and ghee. Serve on a bed of sautéed spinach with plump sherry-soaked raisins for an easy showstopper.

INGREDIENTS

½ cup black raisins

⅓ cup sherry

16 large sea scallops

Kosher salt to taste

Freshly ground black pepper to taste

1 tablespoon ghee

1 tablespoon unsalted butter

2 shallots, minced

4 cloves garlic, minced

1 pound baby spinach

½ cup pine nuts, toasted

Place the raisins and sherry in a small bowl and plump for 20 minutes, then drain and discard the sherry.

Rinse the scallops with cold water and thoroughly pat dry. Season with salt and pepper.

Heat about two thirds of the ghee and all of the butter in a large cast-iron skillet over medium-high heat. Gently add the scallops to the skillet, making sure they are not touching one another. Cook for 2 minutes undisturbed. The underside should have a golden crust. Turn the scallops gently and sear for an additional 2 minutes on the other side. The scallops should still be translucent in the center. Remove from the pan and keep warm.

Add the remaining ghee to the skillet. Add the shallots and garlic and cook, stirring constantly, for 30 seconds. Add the spinach and toss until it is wilted. Add the drained raisins and pine nuts. Toss to combine.

Divide the spinach among four plates. Top each portion with 3 or 4 scallops and serve immediately.

MOROCCAN MEATLOAF

Serves 6 to 8 as a main course

This tender and juicy meatloaf recipe is an adaption of an adaptation. First conceived by cookbook author Ruth "Miss Ruby" Adams Bronz, it was later revised by Marialisa Calta for *The New York Times*. My interpretation showcases many of the fabulous flavors that characterize Moroccan cuisine.

INGREDIENTS

2 pounds lean ground lamb

8 ounces ground beef

2 large eggs

¼ cup whole milk

½ cup rolled oats

2 cloves garlic, minced

1 small yellow onion, finely diced

1 ½ teaspoons kosher salt

1 teaspoon freshly ground black pepper

½ teaspoon harissa powder

1 teaspoon ground allspice

1 teaspoon dried thyme

½ teaspoon ground cumin

¼ teaspoon ground cinnamon

1 tablespoon minced orange zest

½ cup pine nuts

½ cup black raisins

3 tablespoons Worcestershire sauce

4 tablespoons unsalted butter, half melted

1 cup minced shallots

1 tablespoon freshly squeezed lemon juice

¼ cup golden raisins

1 teaspoon dried thyme

½ teaspoon ground allspice

3 cups diced canned tomatoes and their juices

Chopped flat-leaf parsley for garnish

Preheat the oven to 425°F. Line a baking sheet with parchment paper and set aside.

In a large bowl, combine the lamb and the beef, mixing well. In a separate bowl beat the eggs, then stir in the milk and oats. Pour the egg mixture into the bowl with the meat. Add half of the minced garlic, onion, spices, orange zest, pine nuts, raisins, and Worcestershire sauce. Mix thoroughly.

Shape the meatloaf into an oval loaf and place it on the prepared baking sheet. Drizzle the meatloaf with 2 tablespoons melted butter. Bake until cooked through, about 1 hour, or to 160°F on an instant-read thermometer. Allow to rest before slicing.

In a skillet, melt the remaining butter. Add the shallots and sauté until soft, 5 to 7 minutes. Add the remaining garlic and sauté for 1 additional minute. Add all the remaining ingredients to the skillet, except the parsley. Simmer, stirring occasionally, until the sauce is fairly thick, about 30 minutes. Pour some of the sauce over the meatloaf and serve the rest alongside in a sauceboat. Garnish with parsley.

SALT

SALT, A UBIQUITOUS STAPLE, is the superstar of my pantry. It can enhance the sweetness of food, draw out nuanced flavors, and balance bitter tastes. Wielded wisely, it makes rich foods taste richer and helps to achieve marvelously moist meat and poultry.

Salting food before taking a bite can offer an up-front explosion of flavor. However, salt added strategically throughout the cooking process is both subtle and powerful. Knowing which salt to use is equally important.

TYPES OF SALT

There are two main sources of salt: from the sea and from rocks. Sea salt has a briny taste and is more complex than rock salt due to the minerals in the ocean. Rock salt, which is mined from the earth, gives a stronger flavor dimension to foods.

There is a wonderful world of salt to explore, from coarse gray salt harvested by hand off the coast of southern Brittany to flaky salt from the chilly coastal waters of the Pacific Northwest.

KNOW YOUR SALTS

Table salt is probably the most familiar salt of all. Harvested from underground salt mines, it is highly refined to remove impurities and trace minerals. Most table salt is iodized.

Kosher salt is the salt of choice for many cooks. It is larger and coarser than table salt and contains no iodine, which can lend a bitter taste. Thanks to its light and flaky texture, it dissolves quickly.

Sea salt is collected from evaporated seawater and is often harvested by hand. Flaky and soft to the touch, it offers texture and brininess that vary primarily depending on its origins.

Fleur de sel (translated as "flower of salt") is a sea salt from the surface of tidal pools in Brittany,

France. It is carefully hand-harvested using special wooden rakes. Delicate, aromatic, and labor-intensive to produce, fleur de sel is sometimes referred to as the caviar of salts.

Flake salt is thin and irregularly shaped. Harvested from salt water through evaporation, it has a wonderful salty taste and low mineral content. The crunchy crystals are best used as a finishing salt.

Himalayan pink salt is harvested by hand from the Khewra salt mines in the mountains of Pakistan. Notable for its blushing color, it ranges from pale pink to deep coral. It has rich mineral content—it contains all eighty-four natural minerals found in the human body—and its flavor is much more complex than that of most kitchen salts.

Black salt, also called kala namak, is a Himalayan salt from Nepal. Before it is stored and aged, the salt is packed in jars with herbs, spices, and charcoal, then fired in a furnace for twenty-four hours.

Celtic sea salt, also known as sel gris, is a gray salt harvested from the circular current of water along the French coast. Unlike fleur de sel, which is combed from the surface of salt water, Celtic salt is raked from the tidal floor. Its large crystals offer a strong, pleasantly briny flavor.

SALT-BAKED FISH

Serves 2 to 4 as a main course

Salt-baked fish is exactly what the name implies—a whole fish encrusted in salt and roasted in a hot oven. Not only is it super simple to prepare, but salt-baked fish is almost impossible to overcook. The salt crust insulates the fish, slows down the cooking, and traps in the moisture. The result is an incredibly flaky and flavorful fish. Since you remove the skin that was in contact with the salt, it's not overly saline, and you do not have to bother to scale the fish. This recipe works well with any lean, white, flaky fish, including black sea bass, branzino, flounder, red snapper, tilapia, and rainbow trout.

INGREDIENTS

3 pounds kosher salt	One 2½-pound whole fish, gutted,
5 large sprigs rosemary	with the head, skin, and scales
10 sprigs thyme	Extra-virgin olive oil to taste
	Fleur de sel to taste

Preheat the oven to 400°F. Line a large rimmed baking sheet with parchment paper and set aside.

In a large bowl, mix the kosher salt with ½ cup water until it resembles wet sand. Strip the leaves from half of the rosemary and thyme sprigs and mix into the bowl of salt.

Spread half of the salt mixture in the center of the baking sheet and top the salt with the remaining rosemary and thyme sprigs. Place the fish on top of the salt and cover it with the remaining salt mixture. Lightly pack the salt to cover the fish completely.

Place the fish in the oven and roast until a thermometer inserted through the crust into the thickest part of the fish registers 135°F, about 35 minutes. Allow the fish to rest for 5 minutes.

Using a small mallet or wooden spoon, gently crack the salt coating. Remove and discard the salt crust and the skin from the top of the fish. Using a fish spatula, carefully transfer the top fillet to a platter. Flip the fish over and repeat the process. Drizzle the fish with olive oil, sprinkle with fleur de sel, and serve.

TUNA

THERE ARE CERTAIN FOODS that send me on a one-way trip down memory lane. One is a pot of beef stew. My mother would always make a pot on the odd chilly day in Texas. But my very favorite comfort meal is tuna noodle casserole. When I am feeling nostalgic, I make the same classic casserole for my own family, although I embellish mine with fresh mushrooms, a splash of sherry, Gruyère, and panko breadcrumbs.

Tuna is one pantry staple that I am never without. There is no question that tuna is a convenient protein when you need a quick sandwich or lunch. From filets in olive oil to water-packed tuna, there are many excellent options.

I love good-quality oil-packed tuna, available in both cans and jars. Even though I tend to prefer glass jars for the cleaner taste, such as Tonnino brand tuna filets, there are some types available in cans that I like, including Ortiz bonito del norte albacore and Genova. Each costs a bit more than other brands but delivers on taste. With meaty, rosy-colored flakes and a clean seafood flavor, the right tuna is delicious on its own with just a pinch of salt and a slice of bread.

TUNA TERMS

Albacore: The lightest color tuna with a firm texture and the mildest flavor, it is also known as bonito del norte tuna.

Chunk: A solid tuna that is packed in varying sizes of both chunks and flakes.

Dolphin-safe: Tuna that is harvested using fishing methods that are not harmful to dolphins.

Light: Typically from either skipjack or yellowfin tuna, light tuna has a soft texture. Despite its name, it is often dark in color.

MSC-certified: Any tuna with this marking from the Marine Stewardship Council has been certified to meet the group's rigorous standards for sustainable fishing practices.

Pole and line caught: Catching tuna one-by-one on traditional fishing lines is one of the most sustainable methods.

Solid: Packed as a single filet, this type is large and firm with fewer flakes.

Tonno: The Italian word for tuna, which appears on solid-packed tuna in oil from Italy.

White: The only species of fish that can be called white tuna is albacore.

Wild caught: This is a widely used marketing term, despite the fact that almost all tuna is wild caught.

NIÇOISE TOAST

Serves 4 as a starter or as a light main course

My spin on the classic Niçoise salad uses many pantry ingredients. Serve with a crisp glass of rosé or white wine.

INGREDIENTS

4 large eggs

4 Roma tomatoes, thinly sliced

¼ cup freshly squeezed lemon juice

1 shallot, thinly sliced

½ teaspoon kosher salt

¼ cup extra-virgin olive oil,
   plus more for drizzling

4 slices sourdough bread

¼ cup basil pesto, preferably Seggiano

Two 6- to 7-ounce jars oil-packed tuna, drained and flaked

¼ cup diced red onion

¼ cup oil-cured black olives, pitted and torn by hand

Flaky sea salt to taste

Freshly ground black pepper to taste

Fresh thyme sprigs for garnish

Place the eggs in a single layer on the bottom of a large saucepan. Add enough cold water to cover them by 2 inches. Over high heat, bring the water to a rolling boil. Once the water comes to a boil, turn off the heat. Cover the saucepan and leave it on the burner for 10 minutes. With a slotted spoon, remove the eggs from the water. Run them under cold water to stop the cooking. Peel the eggs, thinly slice, and set aside.

Gently toss the tomatoes with the lemon juice, shallot, and kosher salt in a medium bowl, and set aside.

Heat 2 tablespoons of the oil in a large skillet over medium heat. Add 2 slices of bread. Cook until both sides are golden brown, about 3 minutes per side. Transfer to a platter. Repeat with another 2 tablespoons oil and the remaining slices of bread.

Spread 1 tablespoon of pesto over each slice of bread. Top each with tuna and the tomato mixture. Arrange the egg slices on top. Scatter on red onion and olives and season with sea salt and pepper. Drizzle with additional oil, garnish with thyme, and serve.

ALBACORE PANZANELLA SALAD

Serves 4 to 6 as a light main course

At the height of tomato season, this salad uses ripe fruit off my vines and bread that I have on hand, including any that is starting to grow stale, as it softens when it soaks up the dressing and the juices from the tomatoes. I include albacore tuna for enhanced richness.

INGREDIENTS

2 pounds ripe tomatoes

2½ teaspoons kosher salt

6 cups 1½-inch cubes ciabatta or other bread

½ cup plus 2 tablespoons extra-virgin olive oil

1 small shallot, minced

3 cloves garlic, minced

2 tablespoons white wine vinegar

½ teaspoon whole-grain mustard, preferably Maille

½ teaspoon freshly ground black pepper

Two 5-ounce cans albacore tuna in olive oil, drained and flaked

½ cup fresh basil, roughly chopped

Fresh oregano sprigs for garnish

Preheat the oven to 350°F.

Set a colander over a large bowl. Cut the tomatoes into small wedges and place the tomato wedges in the colander. Season the tomatoes with 2 teaspoons of the salt and toss to coat. Allow the tomatoes to drain at room temperature for 20 minutes, gently tossing occasionally.

In a large bowl, mix the bread cubes with 2 tablespoons of the oil. Transfer the bread to a rimmed baking sheet. Bake until the bread is crisp and golden-brown, about 15 minutes. Remove the bread from the oven and allow to cool.

Remove the colander from the bowl and save the accumulated tomato juice. Add the shallot, garlic, vinegar, and mustard to the bowl of tomato juice. Whisking constantly, pour in the remaining ½ cup oil in a thin stream. Season the dressing with the remaining ½ teaspoon salt and the pepper.

In a large serving bowl combine the toasted bread cubes, tomatoes, and tuna with the dressing. Add the basil leaves. Toss again to coat evenly. Let the salad stand at room temperature for 30 minutes before serving, gently tossing occasionally, to allow the bread to absorb the dressing. Garnish with fresh sprigs of oregano and serve.

ARUGULA, FETA, AND WHITE BEAN TUNA SALAD

Serves 4 to 6 as a light main course

This sublime salad is a great pantry standby. Perfect for a weekend lunch or a quick weeknight dinner, it is packed with flavor and can be prepared in minutes. With so few ingredients, though, what is included needs to be great. Be sure to use good-quality tuna, olives, and oil for the most flavor.

INGREDIENTS

¼ cup extra-virgin olive oil

2 tablespoons red wine vinegar

1 tablespoon freshly squeezed lemon juice

½ teaspoon sea salt

½ teaspoon freshly ground black pepper

1 tablespoon diced shallot

1 teaspoon whole-grain mustard

Two 5-ounce cans albacore tuna in oil, drained and flaked

One 15-ounce can great northern beans, rinsed and drained

1 small red onion, thinly sliced

⅓ cup chopped Kalamata olives

¾ cup sundried tomatoes in olive oil, drained and julienned

3 cups arugula

4 cups red leaf lettuce

1 cup crumbled feta cheese

In a small bowl, whisk together the oil, vinegar, lemon juice, salt, pepper, shallot, and mustard until well blended and emulsified.

Place the tuna, beans, onion, olives, sundried tomatoes, arugula, and red leaf lettuce in a large bowl. Drizzle the salad with the vinaigrette and gently toss to coat. Top with feta cheese and serve.

UDON

NOODLES ARE A BELOVED COMFORT FOOD in many cultures. From a classic plate of Italian cacio e pepe to a bowl of Vietnamese pho to brothy udon, they are deliciously soothing.

Udon, thick chewy Japanese noodles, are customarily served in soup or with a dipping sauce. They are one of the three most popular noodles in Japan (the two others are soba and ramen). Made from wheat flour, salt, and water, udon are enjoyed both hot and chilled. Either way, they should be rinsed under cold water to remove the surface starch that can make them gummy. Depending on the region, the basic ingredients and techniques may vary slightly, but the results are always delicious.

POPULAR UDON DISHES

Kake udon is the most well-known udon dish. Comprised of noodles and a hot broth made from dashi, soy sauce, and mirin, as well as scallions, it is included on many Japanese menus.

Miso nikomi udon is a robust soup that is flavored with red miso paste and served in a light broth. Rich and warming, it is jam-packed with vegetables and may include chicken, eggs, fish, or tofu.

Udon suki is a cross between pho and a seafood-laden bouillabaisse. A personal favorite, it is made with an assortment of ingredients, such as tiger shrimp, squid, eel, clams, salmon, and shiitake mushrooms. The stock is flavored with a sweet and savory miso.

Yaki udon is a staple in many Japanese pubs. Stir-fried noodles are loaded with shredded meat, julienned vegetables, and soy sauce. Fast and easy to make, it is often consumed as a late-night snack.

Tsukimi udon is served to celebrate the much-loved Japanese custom of moon viewing each year in mid-autumn. The classic udon dish is topped with a poached egg symbolizing the harvest moon.

SIMPLE UDON SOUP

Serves 2 as a main course

6 ounces udon
4 cups dashi (Japanese fish stock)
2 tablespoons mirin
2 tablespoons soy sauce
¼ teaspoon sea salt
I teaspoon grated fresh ginger
I scallion, white and pale green parts thinly sliced

In large stockpot bring a full pot of water to a rolling boil. Add the noodles and cook until tender, 10 to 12 minutes.

Meanwhile, in a medium saucepan combine the dashi, mirin, soy sauce, and salt and bring to a boil. Reduce the heat to a simmer.

Drain the noodles in a colander and rinse them well under cold water, then drain again. Divide the udon between two deep bowls. Pour the simmering broth over the noodles and top with grated ginger and scallion.

COLD UDON SALAD WITH GARLIC-PEANUT DRESSING

Serves 4 as a main course

Thanks to the creamy peanut dressing, fresh citrus juices, fish sauce, and garlic, this cold salad is bursting with flavor. Packed with shredded cabbage and carrots, thick udon noodles, and rotisserie chicken, it is ideal for picnics, barbecues, and simple suppers.

INGREDIENTS

¼ cup natural creamy peanut butter

¼ cup soy sauce or Bragg liquid aminos

¼ cup rice vinegar

¼ cup freshly squeezed orange juice

3 tablespoons freshly squeezed lime juice

3 tablespoons Thai fish sauce

2 tablespoons honey

2 cloves garlic, roughly chopped

¼ cup grapeseed oil

2 tablespoons toasted sesame oil

½ teaspoon kosher salt

¼ teaspoon red pepper flakes

8 ounces dried udon noodles

2 cups shredded rotisserie chicken

1 cup shredded carrots

1 cup shredded purple cabbage

1 cup shredded green cabbage

2 teaspoons sesame seeds, toasted

½ cup lightly salted peanuts, chopped

Combine the peanut butter, soy sauce, vinegar, juices, fish sauce, honey, garlic, oils, salt, and red pepper flakes in a blender. Blend until emulsified and creamy, then set aside.

In large stockpot bring 4 gallons of water to a rolling boil. Add the noodles and cook until tender, 10 to 12 minutes. Drain the noodles in a colander, rinse them under cold water, and drain them again.

In a large bowl, toss the well-drained noodles with the chicken, carrots, and cabbages. Add about three quarters of the dressing and toss to coat evenly.

Refrigerate the salad for 15 minutes. Then drizzle over the remaining dressing and top with the sesame seeds and peanuts. Serve immediately.

VINEGAR

VINEGAR IS ONE OF THE MOST USEFUL INGREDIENTS in the kitchen arsenal. If you want to brighten your food, provide additional depth, or just add an acidic kick, all you need is a splash of vinegar.

From sweet and sour rice wine vinegar to syrupy balsamic vinegar, this flavorful acid offers much more than just a backbone for vinaigrette. Like salt and citrus, vinegar can exalt all the other ingredients in a dish. It emboldens bland soups, gives stews more structure, and lifts the flavor of roasted vegetables.

There are many fun and notable varieties to explore. From California golden balsamic vinegar produced by Sparrow Lane to black garlic vinegar produced by New York City-based Ramp Up, there is something for everyone.

TYPES OF VINEGAR

Here is a roundup of a few essential vinegars that should grace the shelves of every well-stocked pantry.

Apple cider vinegar is a must-have in the kitchen. From stews to stir-fries to slow cooked pork and spicy chutneys, it livens up flavor. It has a profile that is sweeter than that of white wine or red wine vinegar. Try substituting it for wine vinegar for a tangy twist.

Rice vinegar is a staple in Asian cuisines. It provides a bit of sweetness and acidity to food, and it makes a delicious dressing when mixed with sesame oil, soy sauce, and ginger.

White distilled vinegar is often dismissed in the kitchen as something simply used to clean the coffeemaker. But do not be fooled: distilled vinegar can add acidity to your cooking without imparting flavor as lemon or lime would. White distilled vinegar is vital to a true eastern North Carolina barbecue sauce and key to tasty Vietnamese pickled carrots and daikon radishes.

Wine vinegars, including those made with red wine, white wine, champagne, and sherry, serve many purposes. With mid-level acidity and subtle sweetness, wine vinegar is perfect for pickling vegetables, deglazing pans, marinating meats, assembling sauces, and creating zingy vinaigrettes.

A BIT ON BALSAMIC

Traditional balsamic vinegar is made only in Reggio Emilia and Modena, Italy, and is always labelled aceto balsamico tradizionale. It also bears the D.O.P. (Denominazione di Origine Protetta, or Protected Designation of Origin) stamp.

Each batch of balsamic vinegar is presented to a tasting commission of five judges for testing and grading. In Reggio Emilia, traditional balsamic vinegar is awarded one of three grades. *Affinato* (fine) is awarded a red cap, *vecchio* (old) is designated with a silver cap, and *extra vecchio* (extra old) is adorned with a gold cap. In Modena there are only two designations, *affinato*, denoted with a white cap, and *extra vecchio*, denoted with a gold cap.

Traditional balsamic is not used for a cooking, as heat will kill its distinctive bouquet. Rather, it is drizzled over dishes such as veal scaloppine, rich risotto, fresh berries, Parmigiano-Reggiano, or creamy panna cotta. This condiment is expensive and dosed out in small amounts.

The commercial version many of us have in our pantries is a good bet for heating and cooking. Labeled aceto balsamico, this mass-market vinegar simulates the flavor and consistency of a traditional balsamic vinegar. It is perfect for enhancing soups, stews, and sauces.

ROASTED SAUSAGES AND GRAPES

Serves 4 to 6 as a main course

Roasted sweet grapes and red onions spiked with balsamic vinegar provide a beautiful backdrop for sausage. I personally like to use a mix of hot and sweet sausages to add depth of flavor and interest. However, you can use any type of sausages in this cozy dish. Pork sausage, chicken sausage, turkey sausage, and bratwurst will all work. This is great with crusty bread, a green salad, and a glass of red wine.

INGREDIENTS

3 tablespoons extra-virgin olive oil
4 links hot Italian sausage, pricked with a fork
4 links sweet Italian sausage, pricked with a fork
1 large red onion, thinly sliced
½ teaspoon fine sea salt, plus more to taste
¼ cup balsamic vinegar

½ cup chicken stock
20 seedless red grapes, halved
2 tablespoons chopped fresh oregano
½ teaspoon freshly ground black pepper
Fresh oregano sprigs for garnish

In a large skillet, heat 1 tablespoon of the olive oil over medium heat. Once hot, add the sausages. Cook the sausages, turning often, until they are browned on all sides, about 8 minutes. Transfer the sausages to a large platter.

Add the remaining 2 tablespoons olive oil and the onion to the skillet. Sprinkle with the ½ teaspoon salt. Sauté until the onion softens and starts to turn light brown, 6 to 7 minutes.

Add the balsamic vinegar and stock, scraping up any browned bits. Reduce to a gentle simmer. Return the sausages to the skillet and add the grapes. Partially cover the skillet with a lid. Simmer, stirring occasionally, until the sausages are cooked through, about 25 minutes. Sprinkle with the oregano and black pepper. Taste and adjust salt. Garnish with sprigs of oregano and serve.

WALNUTS

NUTS ARE A POPULAR INGREDIENT AROUND THE WORLD, not only for their terrific taste, but for their many health benefits. One of the healthiest and most versatile is the walnut. With its earthy flavor, the walnut lends richness to winter salads and makes cinnamon rolls taste even more decadent.

The two predominant types are the English walnut and the black walnut. Originating in the Middle East, English walnuts are also called Persian walnuts. Their meat is light gold in color and has a mild flavor. They also have a soft exterior that makes them easy to shell.

Black walnuts are native to the United States. The most popular variety is the California black walnut. They are darker in color with a more pronounced flavor and harder shells.

When selecting whole walnuts, look for clean shells with no blemishes, holes, or cracks. Shake the shell; if you can hear the nut rattling inside the shell it is old and dry. For shelled nuts, look for nuts that are plump and unbroken, never discolored or shriveled. Fresh walnuts smell nutty and taste sweet.

Walnuts will remain fresh for up to three months refrigerated and up to one year in the freezer. Walnuts will go rancid when exposed to warm temperatures for long periods of time.

PECANS VERSUS WALNUTS

Pecans and walnuts are in the same family of trees and are sometimes interchangeable in recipes. However, they are two distinctly different fruits, each with its own singular taste. Pecans are sweeter than walnuts, while walnuts offer a buttery flavor.

COOKING WITH WALNUTS

Sautéed leeks, goat cheese, and toasted walnuts over store-bought puff pastry makes a flavorsome main course or weekend lunchtime treat.

A salad of carrots, mandarin oranges, burrata, and walnuts provides a ton of flavor, color, and texture.

A vegetable ragout of eggplants, tomatoes, garlic, Puy lentils, and walnuts is marvelous over mounds of buttery polenta.

Switch out your Sunday roast chicken for quail in a sauce of sweet figs, brandy, and nutty walnuts.

A rich beef stew with pickled walnuts and dark Scottish oatmeal stout is a real winter warmer.

Warm spaghetti tossed with olive oil, raisins, Parmigiano, walnuts, and flat-leaf parsley is sublime and super simple for supper.

A fig, walnut, and blue cheese tart is yummy with a salad, or serve it as an alternative to dessert, just as you would a cheese course.

TOASTED WALNUT SALAD WITH BLUE CHEESE AND PROSCIUTTO

Serves 4 as a side dish

In Italy, insalata del campo is typically a foraged mix of young leaves and shoots. You may not have the opportunity to forage your own greens, but you can make an excellent facsimile. For this salad, greens can include endive, dandelion, arugula, beet greens, oak leaf lettuce, radicchio, spinach, sorrel, or frisée. Be sure to include at least one bitter variety in the mix that will stand up to the bold flavors of the walnuts and blue cheese. Frisée, arugula, and radicchio are all good options.

INGREDIENTS

1 cup walnuts
⅓ cup extra-virgin olive oil
3 tablespoons white balsamic vinegar
½ teaspoon kosher salt

1 teaspoon freshly ground black pepper
8 cups mixed tender greens
6 to 8 slices prosciutto
4 small wedges of semi-hard blue cheese, such as Danish blue

In a dry skillet, toast the walnuts over a medium-low heat, stirring frequently, until fragrant, about 4 minutes. Allow the walnuts to cool. Transfer the nuts to a chopping board. Coarsely chop and set aside.

Whisk together the olive oil, vinegar, salt, and pepper. Place the greens in a large bowl. Drizzle with the vinaigrette and toss to coat evenly. Divide the salad among four plates. Top each salad with slices of prosciutto, a wedge of blue cheese, and ¼ cup of the toasted walnuts. Serve immediately.

PERSIAN DILL AND WALNUT FRITTATA

Serves 4 to 6 as a main course

This is a nourishing dish that can be served as an appetizer, a side dish, or a main course and is good any time of the day. Also known as kuku sabzi, this green goddess is a traditional Persian omelet. Herbs, not eggs, are the star of this dish. While fresh dill, parsley, mint, cilantro, and chives are typically used, you can substitute scallions, tarragon, or any other herbs you have on hand. I personally like mine heavy on the dill and light on the parsley.

INGREDIENTS

6 large eggs, beaten

1 teaspoon rosewater

4 cloves garlic, minced

1 tablespoon unbleached all-purpose flour

½ teaspoon ground turmeric

1 teaspoon kosher salt

½ teaspoon freshly ground black pepper

1 cup chopped fresh dill

½ cup chopped fresh mint

½ cup chopped flat-leaf parsley

½ cup chopped toasted walnuts

3 tablespoons dried cranberries

2 tablespoons ghee

A mix of fresh herbs for garnish

Preheat the oven to 400°F.

Whisk together the eggs, rosewater, garlic, flour, turmeric, salt, and pepper. Stir the herbs, walnuts, and cranberries into the egg mixture. Heat the ghee in a 10-inch cast-iron skillet over medium heat. Pour the egg mixture into the skillet. Cook until the eggs start to set around the edges, 2 to 3 minutes.

Place the skillet in the preheated oven and bake until the eggs are completely set, about 6 to 8 minutes. To check, cut a small slit in the center.

Garnish with fresh herbs. Cut into wedges and serve hot, warm, or cold.

APPLE, WALNUT, AND CASTELVETRANO CHUTNEY

Makes about 2 cups

I love this sweet and savory chutney in the fall when apples are at their peak. Toasted walnuts add a delightful crunch and the salty bite of Castelvetrano olives offers a delicious surprise. While the Aleppo pepper is optional, I would not leave it out of the mix unless you truly cannot tolerate its mild heat. It has a salty flavor with subtle notes of raisin and pomegranate that makes it perfect for chutney. Full of spice, this chutney is wonderful slathered on a slice of warm, crusty bread or served alongside a pork tenderloin. It also couples well with cheese, cold meats, and ham. It is superb sandwiched with cheddar in a grilled cheese.

INGREDIENTS

5 whole cloves

5 whole allspice berries

5 pink peppercorns

2 teaspoons coconut oil

2 shallots, cut into small dice

2 cloves garlic, minced

2 large Granny Smith apples, peeled, cored, and diced

3 tablespoons dark brown sugar

3 tablespoons apple cider vinegar

1 teaspoon brown mustard seeds

½ teaspoon kosher salt

½ cup chopped pitted Castelvetrano olives

½ cup chopped toasted walnuts

¼ cup raisins

½ teaspoon Aleppo pepper

Cut a small square of double-layered cheesecloth or muslin. Place the cloves, allspice berries, and peppercorns in the center of the cloth. Gather the edges and tie the bundle with a piece of string or butcher's twine.

Warm the oil in a medium saucepan over medium heat. Add the shallots and cook, stirring occasionally, until softened, 2 to 3 minutes. Add the garlic and cook, stirring constantly, until fragrant, about 30 seconds. Add the apples, brown sugar, vinegar, mustard seeds, and salt. Add the spice bundle to the saucepan and bring to a boil. Cover and reduce the heat to medium-low. Simmer for 10 minutes.

Uncover the saucepan and increase the heat to medium. Cook, stirring occasionally, until the fruit breaks down and mixture is very soft, 15 to 20 minutes. Remove the chutney from the heat. Remove and discard the spice bundle. Stir in the olives, walnuts, raisins, and Aleppo pepper. Serve warm or at room temperature. Refrigerate any leftovers for up to 2 weeks.

PAN-SEARED WILD SALMON WITH WALNUT-PEAR SALAD

Serves 4 as a main course

Pan-searing is my go-to cooking method for salmon. Tender salmon with crispy skin pairs perfectly with pears, buttery walnuts, and a tangy vinaigrette. Both refreshing and filling, this is a quick and easy dinner.

INGREDIENTS

3 tablespoons finely chopped toasted walnuts

¼ cup grated Parmigiano Reggiano

3 tablespoons freshly squeezed lemon juice

2 tablespoons white balsamic vinegar

2 teaspoons honey

2 teaspoons whole grain mustard

½ clove garlic, minced

½ teaspoon kosher salt

3 tablespoons extra-virgin olive oil

Four 6-ounce wild salmon filets with skin

¼ teaspoon freshly ground black pepper

2 pears

4 cups baby spinach

¼ cup walnut halves

¼ cup crumbled goat cheese

Preheat the oven to 425°F.

In a small bowl combine the toasted walnuts, 2 tablespoons of the Parmigiano Reggiano, 2 tablespoons of the lemon juice, vinegar, honey, mustard, garlic, and ¼ teaspoon of the salt. Add 2 tablespoons of the oil in a thin stream while whisking to incorporate. Set aside.

Sprinkle the salmon with the remaining ¼ teaspoon salt and the pepper. Heat the remaining 1 tablespoon oil in a large cast-iron skillet over medium-high heat. Once the pan is hot, add the salmon skin-side down. Cook without moving until the skin begins to brown, about 3 minutes. Transfer the skillet to the preheated oven. Roast to desired doneness, 5 to 6 minutes, or until just opaque in the center. Remove from the oven.

Core and slice the pears. Toss the slices with the remaining 1 tablespoon lemon juice in a small bowl. In a large bowl, toss the spinach and the prepared vinaigrette. Whisk briefly again if the vinaigrette has separated. Evenly divide the spinach among four plates. Top each portion of salad with a salmon fillet and some of the pears. Garnish with the walnut halves and the goat cheese. Serve immediately.

XO SAUCE

MOST ASIAN SEASONINGS ARE DEEPLY ROOTED in both history and regional cuisine. Fish sauce, a staple ingredient in East and Southeast Asian dishes, has enhanced the taste of food since the fourth century, while gochujang, a savory fermented red chili paste, was introduced into Korean cooking in the fifteenth century. By comparison, XO sauce is a relatively recent condiment, with quite an interesting background.

The Peninsula Hotel on the Kowloon Peninsula in Hong Kong is often credited with inventing XO sauce in the 1980s. However, there is a contingent that believes the seafood restaurants in the Tsim Sha Tsui district of Kowloon were the likely creators. Although no spirits or alcohol are included in the ingredient list, the name is a nod to XO (extra old) cognac and an attempt to ride on the coattails of XO cognac's reputation as a favorite of the affluent.

Dubbed the "caviar of the Orient," XO sauce has become synonymous with Cantonese cooking. It was once difficult to find in the United States, but there are now several popular brands available online and at Asian food markets, among them Lee Kum Kee, Morning Sky, and Meal of Emperor. Though XO sauce is pricey, a little goes a long way, and it will keep in the refrigerator for up to two years.

Recipes for XO sauce vary, but the consistent must-haves are dried scallops, dried shrimp, and smoky ham. Many chefs zealously guard their recipes, while others offer their premium sauces only to their most valued clients. The sauce often incorporates chili pepper, garlic, and oil, making it a flavor bomb with a bewitching umami taste.

FOOD PAIRINGS

XO sauce elevates the inherent flavors of most foods, from crudités and scrambled eggs to steamed fish, ribs, and chicken. Try these XO sauce suggestions:

Toss the sauce with soba noodles, then top with peanuts and bean sprouts.

Mix the sauce with roasted broccoli and toasted sesame seeds.

Toss the sauce with warm green beans and hot bacon.

Spoon a bit onto a bowl of grits and shrimp.

Add the sauce to mussels and serve over a bed of glass noodles.

Drizzle the sauce on a plate of grilled scallops.

CLAMS WITH GARLIC TOAST AND XO SAUCE

Serves 2 as a main course

There are few things more satisfying than a large, steaming hot bowl of fragrant clams. However, they are even more delectable when paired with the complex flavor of XO sauce and the sweet salinity of prosciutto. Toasted garlic bread is a fantastic foil to this savory and briny dish, and it is perfect for dipping.

INGREDIENTS

¼ cup extra-virgin olive oil

⅓ cup chopped scallions, white parts only

3 cloves garlic, minced

1½ cups dry white wine

1 tablespoon XO sauce

2 pounds littleneck or Manila clams, purged and scrubbed

3 tablespoons freshly squeezed lemon juice

Kosher salt to taste

Freshly ground black pepper to taste

4 thick slices sourdough bread

2 cloves garlic, halved

4 slices prosciutto

1 tablespoon chopped flat-leaf parsley

In a large stockpot, heat 2 tablespoons of the olive oil over medium-high heat. When the oil is warm, add the scallions and garlic. Sauté for 1 minute, stirring to avoid browning the garlic.

Pour in the wine and raise the heat to high. Stir in the XO sauce and add the clams. Cover and cook, stirring once or twice, until all the clams have opened, 8 to 10 minutes. Discard any unopened clams. Taste the broth and adjust seasonings. Turn off the heat and keep the pot covered.

Add the remaining 2 tablespoons oil to a large skillet over medium-high heat. Add the bread and toast it, turning, until golden brown on both sides. Rub both sides of the bread with garlic and set aside.

Ladle the clams and their broth into two large soup bowls. Serve with the garlic toast, prosciutto, and fresh parsley.

YUZU

WITH KNOBBY SKIN, A BUMPY TEXTURE, and an uneven shape, yuzu resembles a sad-looking lemon. Prized for its aromatics, it has a smell and taste similar to those of a mandarin orange, grapefruit, or tart lemon. A cut to the green-yellow rind releases its fascinating fragrance. While this sour citrus fruit grows wild throughout central China and Tibet, it is most widely used in Japan.

In Japanese cuisine, yuzu is used as a souring agent in many recipes. However, it is too bitter to be eaten on its own. The zest of the fruit garnishes a variety of dishes, while the juice is used as a seasoning. It is an excellent marinade or a substitute for soy sauce. To protect American crops from diseases, fresh yuzu cannot legally be imported into the United States. Currently yuzu trees are grown in California and their fruit can be found at local farmer's markets, select online retailers, and at specialty and Asian markets. Because of its scarcity, yuzu fetches high prices, and wholesalers tend to be secretive about their sources. The shipment of any yuzu is currently prohibited in Arizona, Florida, Georgia, Louisiana, Texas, and Hawaii. However, yuzu juice is available online and in specialty markets.

PONZU SAUCE

The juice from yuzu is the integral ingredient in Japan's beloved ponzu sauce. Traditionally this sauce is made by simmering rice wine, rice vinegar, soy sauce, bonito flakes, and seaweed, then adding a splash of yuzu juice. It is salty, bitter, sweet, and sour all at once. Perfect tossed with summer vegetables, ponzu sauce is also excellent drizzled over grilled seafood. A great dip for dumplings or pot stickers, it also brings a certain zing to stir-fries. These are some of my favorite ways to use ponzu:

Whisked into a vinaigrette it dresses up leafy greens, pairs beautifully with raw vegetables, and adds depth to an Asian-inspired cabbage salad.

With its citrusy notes, ponzu sauce gives a kick to all kinds of marinades. From pork to beef, it imparts a ton of flavor while tenderizing the meat in the process.

For an unexpected treat, serve it alongside a mignonette sauce and horseradish as an accompaniment to raw oysters.

PONZU-STYLE CITRUS SAUCE

Makes ½ cup

Although this sauce does not have the depth of flavor of a traditionally made ponzu sauce, it is tasty and easy to make with ingredients from the pantry. Because of the difficulty and expense of obtaining yuzu in the United States, I have provided the option of using yuzu juice or replacing it with a mix of other citrus.

2 tablespoons rice vinegar
½ cup mirin
½ cup yuzu juice, or equal parts freshly squeezed lemon and lime juice
½ cup light soy sauce or coconut aminos
1½ teaspoons brown sugar

Whisk together the vinegar, mirin, yuzu juice or citrus juices, soy sauce, and brown sugar in a small bowl.

Let the sauce sit at room temperature for 1 hour to allow the flavors to marry. Cover and refrigerate for up to 3 days.

PAN-SEARED SALMON WITH PONZU-MUSTARD GLAZE

Serves 6 as a main course

This is my favorite method for preparing salmon. With a golden amber crust and a juicy tender center, pan-seared salmon goes from wonderful to wow with a bit of heat. Accompany with a bed of grains and a fresh salad for a quick and easy dinner.

INGREDIENTS

¼ cup Ponzu-style Citrus Sauce (see page 243)

3 tablespoons mirin

2 tablespoons sherry vinegar

1 tablespoon whole-grain mustard, such as Maille

2 teaspoons cornstarch

¼ cup dark brown sugar

2 tablespoons grapeseed oil

Six 5-ounce center-cut salmon filets with skin

Whisk together the ponzu sauce, mirin, vinegar, mustard, 2 tablespoons water, cornstarch, and brown sugar in a small saucepan.

Once the sugar and cornstarch are dissolved, place the saucepan over high heat. Bring to a boil, then reduce the heat to low. Simmer until thick, about 1 minute. Cover the saucepan with a lid and set aside.

Heat the oil in a large nonstick skillet over medium-high heat. Once the oil is hot, place the salmon skin-side up in the skillet. Cook until golden brown, about 5 minutes. Carefully turn the fish with a large spatula, reduce the heat to medium, and cook to desired doneness, 3 to 4 additional minutes for just opaque in the center.

Spoon the ponzu-mustard glaze over the salmon. Transfer the filets to plates or a platter and serve immediately.

ZA'ATAR

AN AROMATIC SPICE MIX that includes sesame seeds and sumac, za'atar has both earthy and citrus undertones. It is most identified with Middle Eastern and Mediterranean cooking. As with curry blends in India, there are hundreds of variations. Many Middle Eastern families have their own unique, sometimes closely guarded, recipes. Za'atar also refers to the wild oregano plant, often included in areas where it grows.

While there is no strictly defined recipe for za'atar, one or more savory dried herbs, such as oregano, marjoram, and thyme, almost always provide a foundation. Toasted cumin, coriander, and sesame seeds may also appear and lend an earthy taste. But the most important ingredient of all is sumac—a tart red fruit that, when dried and ground, imparts a lemony flavor.

ZA'ATAR USES

From roasted chicken to grilled seafood, za'atar is great for seasoning meats.

Sprinkle the spices into a bowl of hummus or olive oil for a delicious dip to serve with flatbread, pita bread, or naan.

Dress up your greens—olive oil, lemon juice, and a dash of za'atar make a great salad dressing.

Dust your pizza or popcorn to add a little zest and spice up the flavor.

SIMPLE ZA'ATAR

Makes ¼ cup plus 1 tablespoon

Za'atar is easy to find in grocery stores and online. I especially love the blend sold by the Spice House. But you should try making your own from scratch at least once. Use this recipe as a starting point and adjust to your own personal taste.

1 tablespoon cumin seeds
1 tablespoon coriander seeds
1 tablespoon dried oregano
1 tablespoon plus 1½ teaspoons
  toasted sesame seeds
1 tablespoon ground sumac
½ teaspoon sea salt
⅛ teaspoon Aleppo pepper

In a small saucepan over medium heat, toast the cumin and coriander seeds until fragrant.

Place the toasted seeds in a mortar (or coffee grinder). Use the pestle to grind the seeds to a fine powder (or pulse the grinder several times). Combine the powder with the oregano, sesame seeds, sumac, salt, and pepper.

Store in a sealed jar in the pantry for up to one month.

BUTTERMILK ROAST CHICKEN

Serves 4 as a main course

This juicy chicken benefits from an overnight bath in buttermilk. Slathered with za'atar, stuffed with thyme, lemon, and garlic, and served atop roasted potatoes, it is the ultimate comfort food.

INGREDIENTS

1 small roasting chicken, 3½ to 4 pounds
2 tablespoons plus 1 teaspoon kosher salt
1 tablespoon plus 2 teaspoons fine sea salt
2 cups cultured low-fat buttermilk
6 large red potatoes
5 shallots, quartered
¼ cup extra-virgin olive oil

1 tablespoon plus 1½ teaspoons sumac
1½ teaspoons freshly ground black pepper
¼ cup za'atar
¼ teaspoon red pepper flakes
1 large lemon, halved
4 cloves garlic
5 sprigs fresh thyme, plus more for garnish

Season the chicken with 2 tablespoons of the kosher salt. Let the chicken sit at room temperature for 30 minutes.

In a small bowl, combine 1 tablespoon plus 1 teaspoon of the sea salt with the buttermilk.

Place the chicken in a gallon-size resealable plastic bag. Pour the buttermilk mixture over the chicken and seal the bag. Distribute the buttermilk to coat the chicken. Refrigerate for 12 to 24 hours. Remove the chicken from the refrigerator and let it sit at room temperature for 1 hour before cooking.

Preheat the oven to 425°F.

Cut the potatoes into wedges. In a roasting pan or 9 by 13-inch glass baking dish, toss the potatoes and the shallots with 1 tablespoon of the oil, the remaining 1 teaspoon sea salt, the sumac, and ½ teaspoon of the black pepper.

Remove the marinated chicken from the plastic bag and discard the marinade. Use paper towels to wipe off excess marinade on the chicken. Season the cavity and exterior of the chicken with the remaining 1 teaspoon kosher salt and the remaining 1 teaspoon black pepper.

In a small bowl, combine the remaining 3 tablespoons oil, 3 tablespoons of the za'atar, and the red pepper flakes, and set aside.

Place the lemon halves, garlic, and thyme sprigs in the cavity of the chicken. Then truss the chicken with kitchen twine. Rub the za'atar-oil mixture all over the skin of the chicken. Sprinkle the skin with the remaining 1 tablespoon za'atar. Place the chicken breast-side up on top of the potatoes. Roast the chicken and potatoes in the preheated oven for 20 minutes. Reduce the heat to 350°F and continue roasting until an instant-read thermometer reads 165°F when inserted into the thickest part of the thigh, about 1½ hours.

Allow the chicken to rest for 10 minutes. Remove the lemon, garlic, and thyme springs from the cavity. Discard the garlic and thyme. Squeeze the juice of the lemons (through a strainer to catch any seeds) over the chicken and potatoes, and garnish with fresh thyme. Carve the chicken and serve with the roasted potatoes.

RECIPE INDEX

ACKNOWLEDGMENTS

Abundant thanks and gratitude to every member of my Facebook cooking club. Not only did you inspire this book, but you contributed your thoughts and time so freely. Your recipes bring great pleasure to me and countless others. With thousands of members, it is hard to thank each of you personally, but I would like to acknowledge a few who share so much advice: Mary Aarons, Carol Barnwell, Marcella Butler, Derrick Crain, Pamela Cortes, Suzanne Costa, Christine Davis, Lonnie DeWitt, Rose Dostal, Kim Driscoll, Cathy Lee Gruhn, Betty Herring, John Oakley Higgins, Nancy Geiger Huslage, Courtney Lake, Alice Lam, Mindy Le, Mairi Mallon, Bill Maltsberger, Nikki Maxwell, Michael Miarecki, Leighanne Mitchell, Larkin Mott, Jodi Veronica Murphy, Jean Plattenberg, Eric Prokesh, Renee Rucci, Mark Shephard, Stephen Simons, Patricia Shutts Spicuzza, Priscilla Teague, Patricia Whiteside, Jim Williamson, and Mila Woody-Daraz.

To Matthew Mead, my creative partner in crime. While you are an amazing photographer, what I value most is our friendship. I look forward to many more projects together.

Many thanks to Wendy Kvalheim, Paul Wojcik, Joseph Marini, James Sparrow, Danielle Eilender, and Rummel Creek Village Antiques for your contributions, which all support the beautiful imagery.

To my editor, Sandy Gilbert Freidus, we did it once again. You truly are the best. I am so happy to call you a friend. As you always say, "Onward." To the exceptionally talented book designers Doug Turshen and Steve Turner. I so much enjoy working with both of you. Y'all never cease to amaze me. Thank you for always taking my ideas and making them even better than I could ever imagine. To everyone at Rizzoli, you are without question incomparable. A special thank you to publisher Charles Miers, copyeditor Natalie Danford, proofreader Tricia Levi, production manager Barbara Sadick, and public relations gurus Jessica Napp, Pam Sommers, and Ron Longe.

A very special thank you to Alex Hitz, Vivian Howard, and Danielle Rollins for your encouragement and thoughtful endorsements.

Matt, Amy, Jack, Michael, and Lea thank you for your enthusiasm. And a huge thanks for taste testing for this book and always lending me a hand in the kitchen. You all make life more fun, and I love you immensely. Thank you to my mom, dad, and sisters for your love and support. Much love and gratitude to my in-laws, Dinah and David Whitaker, for always taking an interest in what I do.

To my wonderful friends who have encouraged my many endeavors—you know who you are and how much I adore you. I am blessed to have so many amazing people in my life, I can only beg forgiveness of those who have supported me over the years and whose names I have failed to mention.

ABOUT THE AUTHOR

RONDA CARMAN is a lifestyle journalist, a former recipe contributor to *Southern Living*, and author of the bestselling books *Entertaining at Home: Inspirations from Celebrated Hosts* and *Designers at Home: Personal Reflections on Stylish Living*. In 2019 she was named to the Salonnière 100, a list of America's best party hosts. Inspired by her time living in Scotland and traveling abroad, Ronda brings international flair to food. In 2020 she launched the Facebook group The Cooking Club.

Ronda has been a guest on Martha Stewart Living Radio, *Good Morning Arkansas*, *Good Morning Scotland*, and *Pittsburgh Today Live*. She has garnered press from publications around the globe, including *Forbes*, *Traditional Home*, *Elle Decor*, *Veranda*, *House Beautiful*, *domino*, *Australian Vogue Living*, *Real Simple*, *Southern Living*, and numerous national and international newspapers.

MATTHEW MEAD is a well-known culinary and lifestyle photographer whose work appears regularly in books, magazines, and Internet campaigns.

First published in the United States of America in 2022 by
Rizzoli International Publications, Inc.
300 Park Avenue South
New York, NY 10010
www.rizzoliusa.com

Author photograph: Nikki Maxwell
Photographer photograph: Jenny Mead

Publisher: Charles Miers
Editor: Sandra Gilbert Freidus
Design: Doug Turshen and Steve Turner
Design Assistance: Olivia Russin
Production Manager: Barbara Sadick
Managing Editor: Lynn Scrabis
Editorial Assistance: Natalie Danford, Tricia Levi, and Marilyn Flaig

Printed in China

2022 2023 2024 2025 / 10 9 8 7 6 5 4 3 2 1

ISBN: 978-0-8478-7156-8
Library of Congress Control Number: 2021948772

Visit us online:
Facebook.com/RizzoliNewYork
instagram.com/rizzolibooks
twitter.com/Rizzoli_Books
pinterest.com/rizzolibooks
youtube.com/user/RizzoliNY
issuu.com/Rizzoli